# Brasses and Brass Rubbing in England

*Left.* Sir Thomas Bullen, KG, 1538, Hever, Kent

*Right.* Sir William de Bryene, 1395, Seal, Kent

# BRASSES
# and
# BRASS RUBBING
# in
# ENGLAND

*Jerome Bertram*

DAVID & CHARLES
NEWTON ABBOT

ISBN 0 7153 5108 7

*Acknowledgement is made to Philip Brown for most of the photographs, my mother, who did the typing, my father and many others for helpful advice, and to the Librarian of Worth Abbey for the use of many books.*

Set in ten on twelve point Times
and printed in Great Britain
by Clarke Doble & Brendon Limited Plymouth
for David & Charles (Publishers) Limited
South Devon House Newton Abbot Devon

# Contents

# List of Illustrations

## PLATES

## IN THE TEXT

*Many of the illustrations of brass rubbings are reproduced from photographs by Philip Brown*

# 1 ✤ Introduction

A many of our bodies shall no doubt
Find native graves; upon the which I trust
Shall witness live in brass of this day's work:
And those that leave their valiant bones in France,
Dying like men, though buried in your dunghills,
They shall be fam'd . . .

*Henry V*, Act IV, Scene 3

I N THE ENGLAND for which King Henry fought, witness does indeed live in brass of thousands of bygone individuals—some who were with him at Agincourt, some famous, and some otherwise utterly unknown. A complete record of English history, the lives and deaths of eight centuries, remains in the monumental brasses to be found in hundreds of parish churches. And yet how few people know anything about them: immediately brasses are mentioned the talk is of brass-*rubbings* and their commercial possibilities. That a brass can and does exist completely separate from a rubbing is a fact that is forgotten; people will even ask how many brass-rubbings there are in a church, and call the Monumental Brass Society (see p 162) the 'Brass Rubbers' Club' or something of the sort.

The *brasses* themselves form a fascinating branch of art that has been largely ignored. They are not only the basis for quaint designs, not only monuments to the dead, not only historical records, but a widespread and greatly varied form of vernacular art, which shares with architecture the advantage of being available for study in situ all over the country and not just in galleries in favoured centres.

So this book describes brasses and everything connected with them, before, in the last chapter, going on to describe what a rubbing is. I have known learned students of brasses who have never done a single rubbing, and collectors of rubbings who have never really looked at a single brass; as well as a host of enthusiasts in between.

A brass, or monumental brass, is a form of monument introduced in the thirteenth century and still occasionally made today. It is composed of sheets of brass—engraved with figures, inscriptions, armorial bearings or other decorations—set into a stone, either as a single plate or with the different parts of the composition cut out and set separately; the stone is laid in a church either as a grave-cover or as a cenotaph—a memorial without a burial. The majority of brasses in England are composed of separate units let into the stone; on some of them, indeed, such as the earliest brasses or the Tomb of the Unknown Soldier in Westminster Abbey, even the letters of the inscription are separately cut out. In the rest of Northern Europe the predominant type is a rectangular plate with the composition engraved on it and the background filled in with decoration. Both types, however, can be found in Britain and on the Continent.

Brasses are most numerous in Britain, with an estimated 8,000, but they are also found in Belgium, Germany, Holland and Poland, with a few examples in most other European countries. The first list of Continental brasses, by H. K. Cameron, has only just been published, and there may be more not yet discovered.

The people represented on British brasses, unlike those on the Continent, cover all social classes from duchesses to small farmers; they include a canonised saint, St Thomas of Hereford, in Hereford Cathedral (Fig 7), and a condemned convict, Isaac Allen, in Lindfield church, Sussex, who died in prison during the Commonwealth. The brasses range from huge memorials, with life-size figures under lofty canopies, a pride of heraldry and a pageant of saints and angels, to simple plates roughly cut with a few 'uncouth rhymes' and naïve epitaphs. These humble, often home-made, memorials are by far the more interesting because they show us a class of society that rarely figures in historical records.

Brasses will interest students of art, history, language, costume and heraldry, and anyone concerned with the lives of his fellow men: some idea of the range of these interests is sketched below, and later chapters will deal more thoroughly with them.

Brass-engraving is a minor art, though many brasses show quite a high standard of design. There are two completely different styles of brass, and to judge them by the same standards, as is usually done, is unfair to both. The earliest brasses consist of thick large plates engraved deeply with a bold line and virtually without shading. The figures are stylised but very impressive; some of the best capture a whole solid entity in a few lines. The posture is standardised—recumbent, with the hands joined in prayer—but the faces gaze at us with a deeply human yet solemnly remote sincerity. Some of these early brasses are surmounted by canopies, imitating the current phases of Gothic architecture, but also drawn simply and forcefully, with no attempt at perspective. Above all, the engraver is faithful to his medium: this is a flat plate of metal, and he treats it as such.

This medieval form of brass was declining in the late fourteenth century and by the beginning of the sixteenth was quite dead. As time went on the engraving tended to become confused, and there was an unsuccessful attempt at a three-dimensional effect by shading and perspective; the figures were usually shown standing, though sometimes still with their heads resting on a helmet or cushion. There are, of course, some good late examples, even from the early sixteenth century, such as Sir Thomas Bullen, 1538, from Hever, Kent (frontispiece), but they are still inferior to the earlier work.

In the middle of the sixteenth century, however, and more markedly in the seventeenth century, came the second style of engraving, smaller but equally interesting, and influenced by Renaissance designs and particularly prints. Some brasses in fact are distinguishable from engraved book plates only in that the designs are not reversed. The figures are shown very much alive, in a variety of different postures and backgrounds. Several fascinating allegorical brasses were engraved in the early seventeenth century, such as those by Richard Haydock in Oxford—two in The Queen's College Chapel, one at New College and one in St Cross, Holywell. The two at The Queen's College are very elaborate: one shows Henry Robinson, Bishop of Carlisle and Provost of the College, in front of his Cathedral and College with various allegorical groups (Fig 26); while the other shows his successor as Provost, Henry Airey, who is likened to Elisha in the inscription, and is surrounded by scenes from the prophet's life. Another allegorical brass, at Shepton Mallet in Somerset (Fig 17), shows a family kneeling round a tomb from which Death is rising to strike down the wife of the family. All these plates recall emblematic and symbolic prints of the period, and differ from the brasses of the medieval engravers in showing a picture instead of an effigy.

Such brasses are unfortunately rare, and most seventeenth- and eighteenth-century brasses are only inscriptions, few of which are engraved with any skill. Their interest lies in their subject. Most of the nineteenth-century brasses belong to the period of the 'romantic revival' and have no artistic merit, while the few twentieth-century examples are rather dull and stereotyped.

Brasses can make history live, though detailed information from them is generally confined to minor characters. The brasses of important historical personages are generally reticent. We know that Sir Thomas Bullen, 1538, at Hever, Kent (frontispiece) was the father of Anne Bullen and consequently the grandfather of Queen Elizabeth I; and that Sir Thomas Vaughan, 1483, of Westminster Abbey, was executed by Richard III; but their brasses give no indication of these facts. On the other hand, later inscriptions do give interesting historical details: for instance, John Price, rector of Petworth, Sussex, is described on his brass, dated 1691, as 'a most faithful helper in the restoration of Charles, who always stood firm on the side of King and Church despite difficult circumstances'. In the same county, at Mid Lavant near Chichester, Hugh May, who died in 1684, was 'Comptroller of the Works to King Charles the Second, Comptroller to the Castle of Windsor and by his Majestie appointed to be Sole Architect in Contriving and Governing the Works in the Great Alterations made by his Majestie in that Castle'.

Brasses are a useful adjunct to the student of history, in preserving details of dress and armour, and the names of men and women who might otherwise be forgotten. Consequently, they are frequently studied in schools.

For students of philology also, brasses are of great interest, as they show the development of language from the fourteenth century onwards. Most inscriptions are in Latin or English; some of the earliest are in Norman French, and show the corruption of that language by the thirteenth and fourteenth centuries. Unfortunately these early inscriptions are usually very short. From the mid-fourteenth century, however, both Latin and English are common and quite lengthy inscriptions are found both in prose and verse. Medieval Latin is often inaccurate and badly spelt: at Findon, Sussex, a rector is commemorated by these lines:

*Obiit octobris Frensche mense die nono*
*Gilbertus anno M septuagesimo bono*
*Ter centum quarto miserere sui Jesu toto*

which can only be translated as 'Gilbert French died on the ninth day in the month of October in the good year one thousand seventy, three hundred and four, Jesus have mercy on all of himself'. Luckily the Renaissance brought a purer form of Latin and some quite good compositions may be found.

English was always more familiar to the engraver, and he was usually accurate, though the English language was just emerging at the time of the earliest English inscriptions, which are contemporary with Langland and Chaucer. But from then on the development of the language up to the eighteenth century can be closely followed. Names developed also: one English county is referred to first as Southamptonshire, then as Hamptonshire and finally as Hampshire.

Another important aspect of brasses is the variety of costume shown—ecclesiastical, civil and military. Although allowance must be made for inevitable stylisation, most of the costumes are reasonably accurate; and in many cases brasses are their only sources. The development of defensive armour, or of ladies' headdresses, may be followed particularly well and stylistic changes perceived even in such standardised garments as priests' vestments. Such features as the rise and fall of the ruff, or the development of men's breeches are also well illustrated, and much else.

Heraldry also plays an important part in brasses and frequently the only clue to the identification of a figure is his armorial bearings. The mere presence of coats-of-arms on a brass will stimulate interest in heraldry, which, in the Middle Ages, was simply the science of identification. On the earlier brasses, when families entitled to armorial bearings were few, the shields are clearly charged with a single distinctive device; but as time passed dynastic marriages produced very complicated combined coats-of-arms and shields with a dozen or more quarterings (Fig 73). Heraldic art degenerated also, as does any art, and one can see the fiery Lions Rampant on the brass to Sir Robert de Bures at Acton, Suffolk, in the early fourteenth century (Fig 8), dwindling into the sickly lions of the eighteenth century. Heraldry was a Gothic art, and did not take kindly to the Renaissance. Relationships can also be traced by heraldry alone, and complete genealogical trees can be worked out from brasses, relating families that may be widely scattered.

Brasses, then, are useful records. Human interest, however, lies in the inscriptions. Take Pett, in East Sussex, dated 1641:

> Heere lies George Theobald a lover of Bells
> And of this howse as that epitaph tells.
> He gave a bell frely to grace the new Stepl'
> Ring out his prayse therefore ye good peopl'

Or take Selmeston, in the same county, dated 1639: 'The body of Henry Rogers, a painefull preacher in this church two and thirty yeeres'; one can only hope that 'painefull' here means 'painstaking'. At Horsmonden in Kent is the brass to Joan Berry, 1604, who 'left behind her 8 sones & one daughter [whose names are listed], of which two last she died in childbed, often utteringe these speaches: Let nether husband nor children nor lands nor goods separate me from the [e] my god'.

Brasses are functional. They are memorials of the dead, part of a long tradition ranging from the Pyramids of Egypt to our own time. Human beings have swung between cremation and inhumation, but it has been a natural instinct of our civilisation to bury the dead decently and mark their graves with monuments. The idea of protecting the body is explicit on the brass to John Sedley and his wife, c 1520, at Southfleet in Kent, where the inscription warns 'Dyg not wityn too Fote of this tombe'. Some people, like Absalom in the Old Testament, have wished to leave some lasting

memory behind them, and have prepared their own tombs. Bishop
Beaumont of Durham, who is reputed to have been utterly unfit for his
office, was determined to outshine his predecessors by the splendour of his
tomb, if he could not do so by his life; and the slab that once held his
magnificent brass still remains in Durham Cathedral.

Many brasses extolling the virtues of the dead were commissioned by
their friends or executors, who usually record what they have done. The
brass to Archbishop Harsnett of Chigwell in Essex (Fig 1), however, carries
the virtue of modesty rather too far: 'Here lies Samuel Harsnett, once vicar
of this church, first unworthy bishop of Chichester, then more unworthy
bishop of Norwich, lastly most unworthy archbishop of York, who died the
25th. day of May, A.D. 1631'. His executor evidently thought the same and
added another inscription stating that 'the Reverend Bishop in his great
humility composed the epitaph'.

A great number of brasses were intended to be reminders of death, often
showing the deceased as a skeleton or wrapped in a shroud. Many of these
were set in position during the person's lifetime, as shown by the unfinished
inscriptions, which left a blank for the date of death. The usual message of
such brasses is:

> *Quisquis eris qui transieris, sta, perlege, plora.*
> *Sum quod eris, fueramque quod es: pro me, precor, ora.*

Or in its English form:

> Whoever ye be that passes by,
> Stop here, and read, and breathe a sigh.
> Look: such as we are, such shall ye be,
> And such as we were, such be ye.

Many of these inscriptions are combined on pre-Reformation brasses with
a plea for prayers, promising spiritual rewards for those that pray for the
dead. Nearly all medieval inscriptions conclude with a prayer, 'on whose
soul may God have mercy'; and even after the Reformation, when praying
for the dead was frowned upon, inscriptions contain a pious wish: 'his soul,
we hope, in heaven doth rest'. Many brasses, however, particularly after the
Reformation, made no reference to any belief in resurrection or after-life,
and some of them seem to suggest that the dead have no hope of life
beyond the grave. Only their memory will remain, preserved by the
monument.

Monumental brasses were designed to mark graves, but they are too often
treated like any other form of art, and moved around, stuck up on the
walls, transferred from church to church and finally lodged in museums,

*Fig 1.* Archbishop Samuel Harsnett,
1631, Chigwell, Essex

which completely destroys the connection they were intended to have with an actual burial. Surely, whenever possible, they ought to be allowed to remain on the graves they were laid to cover.

Few can look at the grisly brass at Oddington near Oxford, which shows a decaying corpse crawling with worms, without at least a shudder, but one need not be at all morbid about brasses. We can learn from their art, their design, their message, and we can even develop the ideas they put forward. Certainly for sheer draughtsmanship there are few models as good as the early fourteenth-century brasses, and modern designers of church vestments are already copying the cut of the medieval vestments they illustrate.

B

# 2 ❄ Making a Brass

ABRASS WAS USUALLY made in accordance with the wishes of the person commemorated on it. Some ordered their tombs to be made long before they grew old; others made combined tombs on the death of their wives; and others bequeathed a sum in their wills towards making a tomb. For those who made no provision at all, friends or heirs would take the initiative. So a tomb may pre- or post-date those buried beneath it. Sir John de Cobham, who rebuilt the church of Cobham near Rochester, Kent, after making tombs for his father and uncle, made his own about 1365, showing himself in armour of the period, holding a model of the church (Fig 32). He did not die, however, until 1407. In the same church, Sir John Brooke laid a brass to himself and his wife when she died in 1506; he did not die until 1512, but the date of his death was never added to the inscription, nor apparently was his figure added to the brass (unless it was laid and afterwards stolen).

The living made their own tombs chiefly to make sure they got what they wanted, and to forestall any possible neglect by their heirs. Also, a standing tomb reminded them they were mortal, as did the gruesome shrouded figures and skeletons shown on many brasses. Brasses bearing the names of the deceased and laid by widow or widower showed the fidelity of the survivor and ensured that they would be buried together; though sometimes the survivor married again and is shown on a second brass with a second partner. The practice of making tombs before death, or at least buying family graves and making additions to the inscriptions, still continues. I have seen a man's grave-stone already prepared beside that of his wife who died a few years ago.

Sometimes wills ordered a tomb and specified brasses, as in the case of William Doddyngton, proved in 1485: 'To be buried in the Charterhouse of London yf I die in the same cite afore the crucifixe over the quyre dor, laying upon me a conveniat stone making mencion by the sidis therof in latyn [ie brass—see below] plate who lieth ther with this scripter upper the middis: *Domine Jhesu fili Dei vivi pone passionem mortem et crucem tuam inter judiciam tuum et animam meam'*. (Quoted in *Monumental Brass Society Transactions*, IX, 469.)

Another instance is the will of James Zouch, who built the great window at the end of the north transept of Christ Church, Oxford, and who desired to be buried in a tomb to be erected under the window which he had built, and for the licence to do so he bequeathed £30 'to the Convent for the vaulting or adorning of that part of the church' and 40 shillings to the prior for his grave. (Quoted in *Monumental Brass Society Transactions*, IX, 511.) The tomb can still be seen, though its brass is now lost.

Brasses laid by friends or executors after the death of the person commemorated are easily distinguished, as those who paid for them seldom failed to record the fact. In St John's College, Oxford, on the brass to John Glover, after a long eulogy we read: *'bene memores amici, ut officiosae pietatis suae testimonium extaret posteris, publicum, et perpetuum mnemosynon hoc aereum curatore Radolpho Huchinsono auctore Thoma Manwaringo utroque et dum vixit conjunctissimo hoc brevi elogio leviter inscriptum, exiguo sumptu, sed infinito studio confectum posuere, Anno Domini: 1578'*—'His friends, remembering him well, in order that a record of his devotion to duty might remain for posterity, placed this public and perpetual monument made in bronze at the expense of Ralph Huchinson, and on the initiative of Thomas Manwaring, both great friends of his during his life, lightly engraved with a short elegy at a negligible cost, but with great emotion, AD 1578'. In the same University, at The Queen's College, on the brass to Bishop Robinson the inscription ends: *'Hoc collegium ipsius laboribus vastitati ereptum, munificentia demum locupletatum istud qualecunque* μνημειον, *gratitudinis testimonium collocavit'*—'This college, saved by his efforts from destruction, and enriched by his generosity, placed this monument as a record of its gratitude'.

Both these brasses were made almost immediately after the date of death, but executors were not always as prompt as that: the brass in Chichester Cathedral to Mayor Bradbridge, who died in 1546, was not engraved until 1592; and the incised slab at Warblington, just over the Hampshire border, to Ralph Smallpage, dated 1558, cannot have been made until c 1590. An extreme case is the brass of c 1440 in Wimborne Minster, Dorset, commemorating King Ethelred of Wessex, who died in 873, but this, like many modern commemorative plates, is an historical record rather than a personal remembrance.

Workshops supplied both the engraved brass and its setting until about 1590, and sent them out fixed together. Thus the brass-engraver had to be a stone-worker as well, and was usually referred to as a 'marbler'. In fact the contract was always made for a *stone*, which was considered the most important part, as the brass was merely to embellish it.

An example of such a contract is that preserved at Antwerp, dated 1536, made between Thomas Leigh of England and Cornelis Hermanszoen (agents for Sir William Sandys) and Arnout Hermanszoen of Aire in Artois (printed in full in *Monumental Brass Society Transactions*, IX, 354). Arnout bound himself to produce two tombs,

> whereof one will be eight feet long and four and a half feet wide; *item*, also four and one quarter feet in height, all Flemish measure, and of Antoing stone; the which tomb to have also on the cover slab a cross of red and white copper beginning at the head and extending the whole length of the stone, and . . . inches wide. And if the said Arnout is unable to get any red copper, he may use white copper, provided that it be of the best quality he can procure. The which cross is to bear in writing these names: 'William Sandys' and 'Margery Sandys', the lettering whereof and the date of the said tomb, to be also of white copper, and three inches wide.

Provision was also made for raised tomb-chests with coats-of-arms, and for the whole to be delivered to Antwerp 'within seven months of the date hereof'; and for the said Arnout to come to England and assemble the tombs, the cost of which was to be thirty pounds Flemish. The Sandys tombs were set up in the chapel of the Holy Trinity at Basingstoke, in whose ruins part of them can still be seen.

Most contracts were, of course, made in England, and Sir William Sandys was exceptional in going to Antwerp for his tomb. Unfortunately, all records of the London brass-workers, including all such contracts, must have been destroyed in the Great Fire of 1666 and very few other contracts are preserved.

*Fig 2.* John Eager, 1641, Crondall, Hampshire

Although most of them were made to order, there are a few cases of apparently 'prefabricated' brasses. At Crondall in Hampshire, near Farnham, the brass to John Eager, 1641, shows a reclining skeleton over a verse, all of excellent draughtsmanship; but the name and date have been very roughly incised, implying that the plate was bought ready made and the name and date added, perhaps by the village blacksmith (Fig 2). It would be interesting to see if there are any duplicates of this plate in other churches.

Other brasses may well have been made up with a 'stock' figure and a new inscription; but generally the whole brass was engraved at the same time, sometimes according to a design specified by the person commemorated, as in the case of the Sandys tombs already described. On medieval brasses the details seem to have been left to the engraver, but by the sixteenth century much more care was being taken by the customer. The correspondence concerning the Gage tombs at Firle near Lewes, Sussex, is preserved at Firle House and shows how particular John Gage was on details of costume. The designer, Gerard Johnson of Southwark, first suggested showing John Gage's wives in the new fashion of farthingales, but this had to be changed to straight gowns to suit John Gage's taste. The hats also were remodelled from an actual hat that was sent up to Southwark to be copied. The sketch (page 67) shows Johnson's original design, with his comments and Gage's all over the margins. The finished brass shows that Gage had his way (Fig 3).

The majority of brasses were probably drawn by hired artists, working for the engravers, according to definite conventions (see Chapter 4). Some seventeenth-century brasses seem to have been designed by artists who normally worked on book-engravings and who may have been specially called in by the workshop to provide a design.

The wording of inscriptions was frequently dictated by the customer, sometimes in a will, as in the examples quoted above. Verses, particularly in the seventeenth century, are often signed: one brass, formerly in Coventry Cathedral, dated 1705, contained twenty verses to a Captain Scrope 'written by himself in the agony and dolorous paines of the gout'. Many brasses, specially after the Renaissance, were set in carved altar-tombs or stone mural monuments, which were commissioned as a unity with the brasses, and designed with them.

Once the design had been agreed on, it had to be executed in the proper materials. The wills and contracts already quoted mentioned 'Latyn' and 'red and white copper'. Both these refer to *latten* or calamine brass, which was an alloy of copper and calamine ore, usually with small amounts of tin, lead and other elements. Modern brass is not made of the same alloy

*Fig 3.* John, Elizabeth and Margaret Gage, 1595,
Firle, Sussex

and is quite different in appearance. Old brass, though technically known as 'latten' (spelt in a variety of ways), was usually called 'brass' from the sixteenth century onwards; it was used for many purposes besides monuments and is mentioned by Chaucer in the description of the carpenter's wife from the *Miller's Tale*:

> And by her girdel heeng a purs of lether,
> Tasseled with grene, and perléd with latoun.

In the Sandys contract, 'white copper' probably means the normal alloy of latten, which is pale in colour; while 'red copper' was an alloy with a much higher percentage of copper, appearing red, as can be seen on some brasses. It was softer than white latten as well as being more expensive and so was less frequently used. The only example I know of the two metals being used together is in Florence, where an inscription before the doors of the Baptistery is made of white latten letters set in a plate of red copper.

During the Middle Ages the metal was imported from Germany already beaten into sheets; but after the mid-sixteenth century brass foundries were started in England which produced thinner plates of a slightly different alloy. In Salisbury Cathedral two brasses side by side, one of the fourteenth century and the other of the late sixteenth, show a very striking contrast in colour between the two alloys.

The agreed design for the brass was traced on to the sheets of metal and probably drawn over in black lead. It was then engraved with a hexagonal-section burin, leaving V-shaped grooves. If an area of the surface had to be cut away for colouring it was cross-hatched with the burin, leaving the lowered area rough. Early brasses were engraved very deeply, and must have been very hard work to produce; several were never finished. At Chartham near Canterbury, on the brass of Sir Robert de Septvans, 1306, only a very small area of the chain-mail was finished, the rest of it being only roughed out. Another early knight, Sir Roger de Trumpington from Trumpington near Cambridge, 1289, has an unfinished shield; the entire background of the shield should have been cut away, leaving the devices standing out, but the work was left after only one cross had been cleared and the rest of the design is only engraved in outline (Fig 4a).

Later the engraving became shallower, and so easier; instead of long deep cuts, closer lines with shading were used. By the seventeenth century most brasses were engraved very lightly, the burin being used more like a pencil than a plough; and some late brasses were probably etched with acid, leaving only very slight lines. After about 1600, areas of the surface were no longer cut away for colouring as they had been before.

Modern brasses and restorations are easily distinguishable from old work, since they are cut mechanically and the lines have flat bottoms instead of the V-shaped grooves left by a burin. Nearly all the lines on modern brasses, however, are still filled in with colouring. The metal also is different, being modern brass, not latten.

Inscriptions were sometimes engraved by the laborious process of cutting away the whole surface, leaving the letters raised. While more attractive than engraved letters, this was a much more difficult job and was consequently rarely done. Very occasionally a whole figure was treated like this, as at Hambledon, Buckinghamshire.

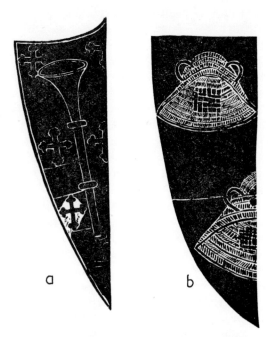

a                                    b

*Fig 4.* (a) Shield of Sir Roger de Trumpington,
1289, Trumpington, Cambridgeshire; (b) Shield of
Sir Robert de Septvans, 1306, Chartham, Kent

When the engraving was finished the figure was cut out of the sheet of brass, and the surplus metal used for small details, such as shields or marginal inscriptions. The long fillets of these inscriptions are frequently made up out of several short strips, as are the thin shafts of canopies or crosses. Large figures also are made up of two or more plates. On the earliest brasses the plates were joined before being laid in the stone; and behind the join a strip of brass was rivetted on to the edge of each plate with a large number of tiny rivets, so neatly done that they can only be seen by looking very closely at the brass itself. Obviously care was needed to align the plates correctly, and the Chartham brass already mentioned is an example of a mistake in this alignment: where the join between plates crosses the shield, there is a misalignment of about a centimetre (Fig 4b). Later brasses, however, do not seem to have been joined before fixing in the stone and there are often wide gaps between plates.

Up to the sixteenth century, after the brass was finished it was usually coloured. Bright pure colours were used, too strong for our tastes; but it must be remembered that all medieval painting was done in such bright colours, and the gentle shades we see on old frescos are the result of years of neglect and burial under whitewash. All the engraved lines were filled in level with the surface, leaving the brass completely smooth. Wherever areas had been cut away, as on shields, heraldic garments or official robes, they were filled in with colour—in some cases real enamel, which has survived almost undamaged on the shield of Sir John Daubernoun, 1277, at Stoke D'Abernon, near Cobham, Surrey; and on the dress of Margaret Gaynesford, c 1480, from Carshalton, near Sutton, Surrey. Most colouring of brasses, however, was done with some softer substance, probably mastic (resin) or even wax, which would be pressed on to the rough bottom of the cut-away areas and into all the engraved lines. Most of the lines were done in black, but probably the grass under a figure's feet was green and the lines of the face perhaps red. Shields, heraldic costumes, official robes and academic gowns were usually in the proper colours, while ladies' dresses and headgear could be any colour. Canopies and other such parts were probably all in black, with other colours on the lancets in the shafts or rose windows in the pediments. Inscriptions were filled in with black, capital letters in red. The silver parts of coats-of-arms and fur on academic gowns or priests' vestments were represented either by a mercury wash or an inlay of lead. The remaining surface of the brass was polished until it shone and it was sometimes actually gilded. Occasionally, instead of cutting-away and filling-in, the surface was painted directly. After about 1600, however, the colouring of brasses practically ceased; apart from a few shields, no more was done than polishing or gilding the surface and filling in the lines with black.

The medieval brass must have been a striking sight in full colour. When we look at a brass now it is usually dull black but when first laid it shone with gold, silver, red, blue and green. Like every other branch of medieval art, a brass was incomplete without its colour and the modern appearance of brasses is due solely to the accumulated dirt of centuries. Brasses on the floor were inevitably walked on, and the colouring matter came out completely, except in the few cases where real enamel was used. Even brasses on the wall have usually lost their colour, as the wax or mastic dried up or was diligently removed by church cleaners. As a result few brasses retain any original colour, though some have been restored. Those that are still coloured are usually on the wall. At Carshalton the brass to Nicholas and Margaret Gaynesford still shows traces of gilding, colouring on the shields and, as already mentioned, the almost perfectly preserved red enamel on the lady's dress. At Isfield, near Uckfield, Sussex, a brass to Thomas and Anne Shurley, 1579, is completely gilded, and the colour remains in all the shields. Two aldermen at St Peter's, Colchester, have red civic mantles, and a few other examples of surviving colour exist, including the famous shield of Sir John Daubernoun.

When the plates of brass had been coloured they were ready to be fixed into their stones. The slab or casement had to be made of an attractive stone that would show up the brass well. Various types were used, but by far the most common was Purbeck marble. Found chiefly in Purbeck, this stone, like the very similar Petworth and Bethersden marbles from the Weald of Kent and Sussex, is a fossil-bearing limestone; when it is cut, the fossil shells show in cross-section, and the whole surface can be polished to produce a very attractive effect. The only disadvantage is that if the stone is subjected to too much pressure it flakes and the whole surface may disintegrate. Other stones occasionally used are slate, black Tournai stone and Ardennes limestone. Several later sixteenth-century brasses are set on old altar-stones, which can be recognised by the crosses at the corners and centre.

The slab could never be smaller than the size needed to cover the grave (however small the brass), and it could be very much larger, up to 16 ft long. The outline of the parts of the brass was marked on to the stone and an indent cut with mallet and chisel, deep enough to sink the brass level with the surface of the stone. When the indent or matrix was finished, several deeper holes were cut at intervals as sockets for the rivets, and holes were then drilled in the brass to correspond with these sockets. It is a peculiar feature of most brasses that little or no care has been taken to position these rivet holes so as not to affect the design; many figures have a Cyclops eye in the forehead where the rivet has been fixed. Only a very few workmen seem to have taken the trouble to make the rivets fit into the design.

The sockets in the indent were then filled with molten lead, either poured in through a runnel across the base of the indent or poured directly into the sockets. Into these lead plugs were set the base of the rivets, which were round pegs of brass, misshapen at the bottom to grip in the lead. When the lead was cool it was consolidated with a metal punch.

The rivets now stuck up through the indent ready to receive the plates. These were positioned carefully over the indent and hot bitumen or pitch was run in under the brass. This was then pressed down, and the rivets were filed off close to the surface and hammered over the brass. Any pitch seeping out at the edges was scraped off. The surface of the brass was then re-finished over the rivets and in a few instances lines of engraving were continued over them. If well fixed the rivets should not have been visible at all.

This was the normal method of fixing from the fourteenth century onwards. The earliest brasses were not rivetted down but held in the stone merely by their own weight, which was fairly considerable, and a bed of pitch. The reinforcing strips behind joins in the brass also served as anchors; these can be seen in position on the brass to Margarete de Camoys at Trotton near Midhurst, Sussex (Fig 9) since there are holes in the figure, in which there were once enamel shields, and through these can be seen the backing-strips. This method of fixing was unsatisfactory, since the brass could easily become loose or be stolen, and so in the mid-fourteenth century the method described above was evolved. Others ways of fixing are occasionally found. At Cranbrook, Kent, is the indent of a figure on an altar-tomb in which remain wooden plugs instead of the lead normally used to hold the rivets. Later brasses, in the seventeenth and eighteenth centuries, were often screwed straight on to a wall. Mural brasses could not, of course, be fixed with molten pitch unless this was done in the workshop, so late mural brasses often have no backing, or, as with a brass in Trinity church, Coventry, a backing of thick brown paper. Many mural brasses are held in place by a stone or wooden frame.

Probably the majority of brasses have been re-fixed at one time or another. Those re-fixed by the Monumental Brass Society are done in the proper way with rivets, but amateur fixers have used many unsuitable methods, often smearing cement on to the surface of the brass, or using iron nails, or large screws, either counter-sunk or sticking out with sharp edges; or, even more obtrusively, round-headed screws. Some brasses have had lead run round them in the belief that this would hold them down. Others, like the Chartham knight, are held down by large iron clamps. The use of iron will almost inevitably cause corrosion, and the whole brass can thereby be ruined.

Many brasses have become slightly loose, usually because the pitch has dried up and lost its grip. Often, too, the rivets work loose, generally through people walking on the brass or standing furniture on it. Sometimes the rivets have started to protrude. When the brasses have worked loose or for any reason have to be taken up, the Monumental Brass Society willingly gives advice, and in some cases actually carries out the work. Brasses should not be re-fixed except by an expert, since special methods of rivetting are necessary and a knowledge of metallurgy is essential. Far too many loose brasses have been clumsily re-fixed or left lying around in the vestry or vicarage until parts are lost or thrown away.

If due care is taken to protect brasses there is no reason for them ever to come loose. Walking on them inevitably loosens them once the bed of pitch has dried up, but this drying-up is easily detectable since the brass sounds hollow when tapped. Ideally all brasses should be protected from anybody walking on them, without, however, going to the extreme of tearing them up and sticking them on a wall. Since they are often in church aisles and it is impracticable to prevent people walking on them, it is best to cover them with soft thick carpeting, or at least with felt. Coconut matting is useless as it will catch pieces of grit and scratch the brass with them, while sheets of rubber are fatal, as the chemicals used in preparing them will corrode the brass seriously.

Where brasses are lost, or have been stolen, the fixing elements are often plainly visible, as in the example illustrated (page 50), from Burton, near Petworth, Sussex. In the indent of the children under the shield can be seen the lead plug, with the marks of the punch where it was consolidated, as well as some of the bed of pitch; while in the indent of the single child are rivets and the runnels down which the lead was poured. The rivets in position appear on the surviving plates. There are also faint traces of colour in the shields, but these do not appear in the photograph.

Where the rivets survive in an indent it is an almost invariable sign that the plates worked loose before being stolen, since the force needed to tear up a well fixed brass would bring up the rivets with it. Surviving pieces of pitch show that the brass has recently been lost, unless, as at Burton, the indent is on the wall, where pitch may survive for a long time. One disadvantage of taking up slabs containing brasses and setting them on a wall opposite a window is that the heat of the sun is enough to melt the pitch, which will run down the wall in long black streaks.

Once the brass was fixed securely in its indent, the surface of the stone was polished and sometimes painted. It was then ready to be transported, as far as possible by barge, and then by waggon, to the church where it was to be placed. Before the mid-sixteenth century this was almost invariably in the floor, or on an altar-tomb, usually covering the place of burial. Since the walls of medieval churches were covered with paintings, the only available space was the floor, but after the Reformation, when the paintings were destroyed, there was room to set up brasses on the walls, or on the vertical back of an altar-tomb against the wall. Many were set, not in plain slabs, but in elaborate marble plaques of classical design. The figures on these would often be in brass and the inscription cut in stone. Large stone canopies or chantry chapels sometimes formed part of the design, involving major alterations to the church.

Figures on horizontal brasses were invariably positioned with the head to the west, as was the body, for, symbolically, the dead would rise again facing east, Jerusalem and the Second Coming. The east was also the end whence God, looking from the altar, would see the figure of the dead. The inscription, however, was for the benefit of the people, and so, wherever it would be awkward for the people to see the brass from the east—as at Hever, Kent, or Ilminster, Somerset—the inscription was set upside down in relation to the figure, facing west. Inscriptions without effigies were commonly laid facing west. Mural brasses usually showed people kneeling towards the east, except husbands and wives, who often faced each other.

It has already been mentioned that many brasses were laid before the death of the people represented on them, and the inscription was left unfinished, with blanks for the date of death. In theory the date would be filled in when the person died, but in fact a great many of these memorials remain unfinished. Some of the many undated brasses may have been laid before the date of death and no space left for a date, the engraver knowing that it was unlikely ever to be added.

Making incised slabs was simpler than making brasses; the design would be traced on to the slab and then incised with a chisel. On some slabs the lines were left as ridges and the space between them cut away; when the design was completed the lines were filled in with a substance similar to that used for brasses. Large areas might be filled in with white cement, and sometimes thin sheets of marble. In Italy many incised slabs became veritable mosaics of different coloured marbles, but in England the use of stone inlays seems to have been comparatively rare. The surface of the stone of some slabs may have been painted, as the designs are very simple and needed more detail. Some late incised slabs seem to have been engraved with a burin, not a chisel, and are designed to be placed on a wall. Some of these were coloured and several were painted yellow all over to simulate brass. The techniques of working incised slabs and brasses were frequently combined, with brass inlays filling important parts in the design of an incised slab.

The stones used for making incised slabs were necessarily hard, able to withstand a certain amount of wear and strong enough to preserve the lines cut into them. Slate, blue liass stone, alabaster and occasionally Tournai stone were used; the blue liass was by far the most popular during the Middle Ages but was superseded by slate in the late sixteenth century. Other stones, including Purbeck marble, were used occasionally, but soft or brittle stones did not survive and hardly more than fragments exist of such slabs. A few inscriptions and figures are incised on large glazed tiles, as at Lingfield, Surrey. After the seventeenth-century ledger slabs replaced real incised slabs; these were usually of slate, deeply cut with a coat-of-arms and inscription, but apparently never filled in as earlier slabs had been.

A question frequently asked is what was the cost of incised slabs or brasses. It is impossible to give an answer in modern terms, but there are a few surviving records of prices. The Sandys contract already quoted gave the price for two altar-tombs with brass inlays as thirty pounds Flemish. The ledger of a Scots merchant, Andrew Halyburton, who was 'Conservator of the Privileges of the Scottish nation' at Veere in Flanders, from 1493 to 1503, includes six accounts for tomb-slabs bought in Bruges for clients in Scotland. It is not stated whether they were brasses or incised slabs, but one is known to have been a brass and a fragment discovered on the back of a brass in Edinburgh may belong to another. The cost of the manufacture of the six slabs, given in Flemish money, was £22 for the one known to have been brass, £6 15s 0d, £5 10s 0d, £25, £8 and £7. This is the expense of manufacture alone; the cost of transport from Bruges to Veere was in addition about a fifth of the cost of the stone. It is not recorded how much transport from Veere to Scotland cost but it must have been considerable. Packing the stones into a ship, the due to be paid to the ship's master, harbour dues at Veere and again in Edinburgh, then unloading from the ship and transport overland to St Andrews, where most of the slabs were destined, must have almost doubled the cost. In Halyburton's time £2 8s 0d Flemish was equal to one pound English, but it is useless to attempt comparison with modern values. Another account for a Flemish brass imported into Scotland, the fine memorial still surviving in St Nicholas, Aberdeen, gives the cost of manufacture and transport to Veere as £87 10s 6d Flemish or £593 5s 4d Scots, in 1622.

It can be concluded that large brasses were fairly expensive, but that costs could vary tremendously. A small brass was within the reach of farmers and tradesmen, while large brasses were not despised by royalty. King Eric Menred and Queen Ingeburg of Denmark are commemorated by a magnificent brass at Ringsted, on Zealand, but there are no impressive brasses to Kings of England, who preferred three-dimensional effigies. In Wimborne Minster, Dorset, is a small figure commemorating King Ethelred of Wessex, as already mentioned; but the only contemporary brass to a sovereign is a small inscription to Queen Katherine of Aragon, in Peterborough cathedral, which is now mutilated and practically illegible.

# 3 ❋ The History and Development of Brasses

THE ROOTS OF the craft of engraving brasses and incised slabs are lost in prehistory, for engraved stones used as monuments over tombs are found from the earliest civilisations. The ancient Egyptians and Babylonians cut beautiful inscriptions, sometimes combined with figures in low-relief, and sometimes on huge statues such as those in the British Museum. Their lead was followed by the Greeks and Romans and hundreds of stone inscriptions, with or without effigies, survive from classical times.

The Romans strengthened some of their inscriptions by setting letters of bronze into the stone. Sheets of bronze were also engraved with lettering, though apparently not as tomb monuments, and the Twelve Tables of Roman Law, engraved on bronze in 450 BC, must be the earliest recorded 'brasses'. Thus the elements of monumental brasses—the incised funerary inscription and the use of metal for lettering—were established before the Christian era. There was little further development, however, until the end of the Dark Ages, when three separate sources developed to produce the monumental brass.

The first of these sources, an indirect one, was the characteristic tomb of an important person during the early Middle Ages: a tomb-chest with a life-size solid effigy reclining on top. This, unlike a classical tomb, was placed inside a church and took up a great deal of space (page 152). As a result less intrusive tombs were made under the church floor and covered by stones with carved figures in relief; several examples can be seen in the cloisters of Westminster Abbey. The next development, which cluttered the church even less, was to make the stone slab absolutely flat, merely cutting the lines of the figure into it, thus evolving what is usually known as an incised slab; examples survive from the twelfth century, a good one being of an abbot from Carisbrooke Priory in the Isle of Wight, c 1180 (Fig 5).

The second source of brasses was the other early medieval form of monument: a cross embossed on the lid of a stone coffin that was sunk

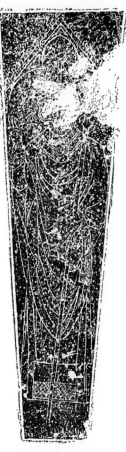

*Fig 5.* Incised Slab: (?) an abbot of Lire, c 1180, Carisbrooke, Isle of Wight

*Fig 6.* Incised Slab: Bishop William Bytton, 1274, Wells Cathedral

into the floor. These were very common, especially in the West of England, and a good series can be seen in the parish churches of Herefordshire. In time these crosses came to be incised into the stone instead of raised above it. This second class of incised slab always retained the shape of a coffin lid, narrower at the bottom than the top, and this became the shape of nearly all incised slabs and brasses in the thirteenth and early fourteenth centuries. Occasionally croziers were substituted for the cross on slabs to bishops and abbots, and some show a carved face in the centre of the cross.

Both types became common in the thirteenth century, with more elaborate designs. There is a crude but impressive example at Sollars Hope, Hereford, to a knight, c 1225, under a cross; and a more sophisticated example in Wells Cathedral to Bishop William Bytton, 1274. Apart from the face, which seems to have been deliberately knocked away, the latter is in good condition, and beautifully drawn; it is cut in a blue liass stone which I am told is so hard and brittle that modern stonemasons are reluctant to use it (Fig 6).

The chief drawback to stone slabs is that they can very easily be worn away by passing feet, or damaged accidentally, or deliberately by vandals (including initial-carvers); and few have survived in such good condition as those illustrated. As a result the engraver turned to a harder material—metal. The third of the sources mentioned was the art of cloisonné enamel, which centred on Limoges: plates of latten were either cut away to leave raised lines or had strips of metal soldered on to make lines, and coloured enamel was spread between the lines. An early example from England is the famous Alfred Jewel, made in the ninth century and now in the Ashmolean Museum at Oxford. These enamels were very small because they were costly to make. They were occasionally set into tombs—for example, into the tomb of Geoffrey Plantagenet at Le Mans, now in the museum there—but they more usually served as small items of church jewellery.

These three sources were finally combined in 1208, when the first recorded 'brass' was laid in St Paul's church, Bedford. It commemorated Simon de Beauchamp and seems to have included a cross, and a figure in metal, almost certainly with enamel on the heraldic parts of his costume. No brass remains, however, and it is not even certain that the indent preserved in the church belongs to it, so it is known only from old references.

THIRTEENTH-CENTURY BRASSES

Two types of brass memorial developed side-by-side throughout the thirteenth century. One was almost a reversion to the classical Roman technique of setting separate letters of brass into the stone, sometimes with an incised cross or crozier in the middle. The earliest surviving brass in England of this type is an inscription in Lincoln Minster, dated 1272, in which twenty-two tiny brass stops remain to separate the words. In Westminster Abbey on two slabs, now unfortunately covered, are preserved a few letters and parts of the stems of slender brass crosses set in glass mosaic: they commemorate two children of William de Valence, dated 1276 and 1277. The extreme delicacy of this type of memorial, however, precluded the survival of any complete examples. The type can be said to have died out in the early fourteenth century, though inscriptions in separate letters were laid up to 1354.

The second style of brass was far more solid, with a whole figure incised

c

on broad plates. The earliest survivor of this type is in Verden near Hanover, to Bishop Iso Wilpe, 1231. Here the design is simply that of an incised slab but in metal. The figure is drawn on a coffin-shaped plate with the background left blank, and the inscription is on fillets of brass. The next example, and the first brass of any size in England, is far more elaborate. It commemorates Sir John Daubernoun from Stoke D'Abernon, near Cobham in Surrey, dated 1277, and he appears as a full-size knight, holding an enamelled shield. There was once an inscription in separate letters, but that has been lost. The drawing of this brass shows a great advance on that of Bishop Iso Wilpe, and indicates that many brasses must have been made during the intervening years to develop the craft to such a point.

A great many Continental brasses were engraved rectangular plates, dispensing with the stone altogether except as a backing, but in England the stone was allowed to show between the various parts of the design, thus making the engraved plates more prominent. From this time onwards foreign and English brass-work developed separately and foreign examples no longer have a place in a history of English brasses. The few foreign brasses imported into England had no influence on English style.

In the last quarter of the thirteenth century many brasses were laid down, but only four survive today and even they have lost their inscriptions. They are full-length armoured figures of Sir John Daubernoun, 1277, already mentioned, and Sir Roger de Trumpington, 1289, at Trumpington near Cambridge; and two half-effigies from Lincolnshire—from Croft near Skegness and Buslingthorpe near Market Rasen (Fig 27)—both c 1300. Fragments survive from other brasses, of which the most interesting is the little figure of St Ethelbert from the brass to St Thomas of Hereford (Fig 7). Thomas Cantilupe, Bishop of Hereford from 1275 to 1282, had been a champion of the barons under Simon de Montfort. He was involved in a dispute with Archbishop Peckham and excommunicated. On his way to Rome to plead his case before the Pope, he died, and his body was sent back to Hereford and buried there. His brass consisted of his figure under a canopy (one of the earliest to be shown on a brass) with an inscription, two fleurs-de-lys, and figures of the Virgin and St Ethelbert, the patrons of the Cathedral. The sanctity of the bishop's life and the miracles worked at his tomb caused him to be canonised in 1320. His body was then transferred to a shrine and the old tomb, still with its brass, left empty. The shrine and body of St Thomas were in due course desecrated and destroyed, except for the skull, which was rescued, but the old tomb remained complete with its brass until the seventeenth century, when the figure and canopy seem to have been lost. From then on various parts were stolen, until, about 1845, the last fragment, a fleur-de-lys, was removed, leaving the indent empty as

*Fig 7.* St Ethelbert, detail from brass to St Thomas of Hereford, 1282, Hereford Cathedral

it now remains. In 1865, however, the figure of St Ethelbert was returned by an ex-choirboy, who had stolen it in 1819; and it is now preserved in the Cathedral's Chained Library.

FOURTEENTH-CENTURY GOTHIC BRASSES

The largest brasses ever made appeared in the first half of the fourteenth century. Huge slabs were decorated with life-size figures under elaborate canopies adorned with saints, prophets, angels and mourners. Owing to the practice of cutting out the design and setting separate engraved units into the stone, the indents, which are all that survive, preserve the outlines and general design of these brasses. The finest of all, and the largest brass that ever existed, was in Durham Cathedral, to Bishop Beaumont, and was laid sometime before his death in 1333. The stone which preserves the indents of this brass is 16 ft long. The figure of Bishop Beaumont in the indent was restored in 1951. Since they were held into the stone by nothing more than their own weight and some pitch, the brasses could easily be removed, and so only a few comparatively small brasses remain, and most of them are mutilated. By far the best is at Acton near Long Melford in Suffolk, commemorating Sir Robert de Bures, who died in 1331 (Fig 8), though the brass seems to have been engraved much earlier, probably soon after Sir Robert became Lord of Acton in 1310. A nineteenth-century mistake gave the date as 1302, but it has been shown in *Monumental Brass Society Transactions*, X, 144, that this is impossible; but on stylistic grounds it cannot be as late as 1331. Its quality of design and engraving is unsurpassed,

Fig 9. Margarete de Camoys, c 1310, Trotton, Sussex

Fig 8. Sir Robert de Bures, c 1310, Acton, Suffolk

and emphasises that with the disappearance of the major brasses of that time we have lost a great treasure.

In the early fourteenth century classes of society other than knights and bishops began to be represented. The earliest surviving ladies, both of c 1310, are at Pitstone, Buckinghamshire, near Tring, and Trotton near Midhurst in Sussex (Fig 9). Both wear long gowns and wimples, Trotton being much more elaborate, with shields and a canopy, now all lost. Parish

Fig 10. Nicholas de
Aumberdene, c 1350,
Taplow, Sussex

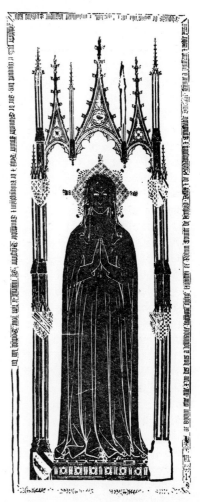

Fig 11. Eleanor, Duchess of
Gloucester, 1399, Westminster
Abbey

priests appear about the same time, the earliest being in Merton College
Chapel, Oxford, dated 1311. Civilians are shown at East Wickham, near
Greenwich, c 1325, but not often before about 1350. By the end of the
fourteenth century all classes of society were represented, including a farmer
and his wife at Rusper near Crawley in Sussex, and a fishmonger at
Taplow in Buckinghamshire who appears in a cross with a fish at the foot
of it (Fig 10).

Later fourteenth-century brasses vary greatly in size: some are very small plates with short inscriptions while others are large and elaborate, though never as big as the earlier ones. They became more solid. Less was cut out of them, and so there were fewer fragile parts to get lost; probably the earlier brasses were already becoming mutilated and the makers drew the obvious conclusion. The method of fixing the plates was improved, as described in Chapter 2.

The larger brasses continued to be excellently made up to the end of the century—they were well drawn, original in design and deeply and clearly engraved—but few remain. Eleanor de Bohun, the Duchess of Gloucester in Shakespeare's *Richard II*, has a beautiful brass in Westminster Abbey, dated 1399 (Fig 11): she is shown in widow's weeds under an elegant canopy which is enriched by fascinating details such as an angel holding one of the shields, a lion and a swan forming the springs of the canopy, and the repeated chained swan, the badge of Gloucester.

One of the most interesting brasses in England is Bishop Wyvil's, 1375, in Salisbury Cathedral. The bishop is shown standing in a castle whose gate is guarded by a fierce-looking Champion, and outside the gate are trees and rabbits. A good deal of history is compressed into this picture. The Castle of Sherborne in Dorset had been taken from the bishopric of Old Sarum by King Stephen and held by the crown until Edward III granted it to the Earl of Salisbury. As soon as the property was out of royal control, Bishop Wyvil began a lawsuit for its recovery. The Earl, thinking to discourage this turbulent priest, demanded trial by combat, to which, however, the bishop agreed, producing a Champion to fight for him. The bishop was nearly disqualified when rolls of prayers were discovered hidden in the Champion's clothing, but after the Earl failed to appear at the appointed time, the case went by default and the Bishop got the Castle. He did, however, pay a considerable sum in compensation to the Earl. The Champion is shown on the brass equipped with the proper weapons for trial by combat: a long war-hammer and a shield with a socket in it. Victory went to the warrior who could catch his opponent's weapon in the socket of his shield, and so disarm him. Because of this formal method of engagement no body-armour was needed, and the Champion is shown in a plain jerkin and hose. The trees and rabbits represent the Chase of Bere, a hunting ground which the Bishop also recovered for the see, though no details are recorded of this case.

A fine brass to a knight, Sir Hugh Hastings, 1347, at Elsing near Dereham in Norfolk, shows him in full armour with the remains of a fine canopy flanked by eight of the highest in the land as weepers (Fig 31). Another brass to one of the nobility is at Ashford in Kent, to Elizabeth, Countess

*Fig 12.* Elizabeth,
Countess Atholl, 1375,
Ashford, Kent
(present condition)

*Fig 13.* Elizabeth, Countess Atholl, 1375,
Ashford, Kent (drawing made in 1628)

Atholl, 1375 (Fig 12). It is unfortunately badly mutilated, and has been relaid in a new stone, so the indents are lost, and were it not for a seventeenth-century drawing (Fig 13) the design would be totally obscure. This brass may be unique in that the figure is holding up its own canopy. Apart from important examples such as these, however, the average brass of the late fourteenth century is rather dull and stereotyped. Three knights at

Cobham, Kent, dated 1354, c 1365 and 1367 are almost identical, except for the church which one holds (Fig 32), and while they are attractive and 'quaint', they are not well drawn. The period was capable of better work.

Towards the end of the century knights are better drawn, but conventional and monotonous. A great number are impressive in their own way, but make little or no advance stylistically. A typical example is Sir William de Bryene, 1395, at Seal near Sevenoaks in Kent (title page).

Smaller brasses in the second half of the century tend to be poor, usually rather bad copies of the larger brasses, sometimes with charm but often without any real value, of which the best are half-effigies, some of which are quite well drawn. Others, however, like the couple at Rusper in Sussex, are deplorable, far below the standard of the larger brasses.

While the craft of brass-engraving developed, so to a lesser extent did that of stone incising. Incised slabs were now, however, limited almost exclusively to areas where there was a hard local stone. It was uneconomic otherwise, for it was only marginally more expensive to make a brass, which was much harder and more durable than stone, than to transport stone and make an incised slab. The design of incised slabs is closely based on the design of brasses, except for the coarser treatment which stone demanded. There was no possibility of fine or close engraving on stone and so the design retained a clarity and sparsity of line which brass-work soon lost.

As well as true incised slabs, a few were still made in which only certain parts were inlaid with brass, or sometimes with a different coloured stone or cement. At Titchfield near Fareham in Hampshire are the remains of a fine early slab of a knight whose surcoat, sword and face have had the surface removed to take some contrasting colouring substances. Another incised slab, at Westwell near Ashford in Kent, had a canopy, inscription and the head of a priest inlaid, probably with brass but possibly with white marble. This type of memorial, however, seems to have been specially vulnerable to wear and its small plates of brass to theft; none now remain complete. Slabs without their inlays can be found at Pyrton, Oxfordshire; and Boston, Lincolnshire, where there are twenty, all very worn.

A more durable form of memorial than either stone or brass, and one practically ignored in books on the subject, was first developed in the fourteenth century in Sussex. The technique was very different from brass-engraving since the memorials were made of iron, cast in a mould of sand, but the result is similar. The earliest, c 1350, is in Burwash church and commemorates John Collins, the first iron-master to cast cannon in Sussex. It consists of a plain cross over an inscription: *'ORATE P'ANNEMA IHONE COLINES'*—'Pray for the soul of John Colines'.

Another early cast-iron slab is at Rotherfield, just a cross without inscription. The use of cast iron for monuments seems, however, to have been very rare until the sixteenth century (see page 48).

## FIFTEENTH-CENTURY DECLINE

In the first half of the century several very large brasses were laid, the most notable at Cowfold, Sussex, to Thomas Nelond, Prior of Lewes, dated 1433. These large brasses are imposing and magnificent, but they have somehow lost the vitality of the best of the fourteenth century. Even the little bears climbing about on the canopy at Cowfold are not really effective. Early fifteenth-century brasses, though competently designed, are as a rule even more monotonous than the late fourteenth-century knights. Many of them are almost exactly alike: in St Albans and Winchester Cathedrals there were brasses mirroring the one at Cowfold, though only fragments of the St Albans' brass survive and none of that in Winchester; and dozens of other brasses, all over England, are so alike in detail, particularly in the face, that it is clear they have been traced from the same design and come from the same workshop (see Chapter 4).

If in the early fifteenth century brasses were well drawn but monotonous, in the second half of the century they lost even their skill in draughtsmanship. A few brasses made in local workshops are original and interesting in design, though rather crude, such as two brasses at Charwelton, near Daventry in Northamptonshire, but most examples are poor in design and exceptionally dull. Convention dominated: clothes were formalised into patterns that hardly changed for fifty years and must have been quite out of date by the end of that period; postures and the wording of inscriptions were standardised. Most of these are merely a variant on '*orate pro anima cujuslibet, armigeris, filii et haeredis cujuslibet, qui obiit quolibet die, cujus animae propicietur deus amen*'—'pray for the soul of so-an-so, esquire, son of so-and-so, who died on such-and-such a day; may God have mercy on his soul, Amen'. These formulas are usually much abbreviated but one hardly needs to decipher them to know what they say.

The lowest ebb of brass-designing was reached by 1500, and the art stagnated until c 1550. In the early years of the reign of Henry VIII a few brasses of some originality were made, but most are of little interest. The exceptions are a number of rather showy heraldic brasses, originally brightly coloured, such as that to the Shelleys of Clapham near Worthing, 1526, and those made for particularly wealthy or important people, notably Sir Thomas Bullen, 1538, from Hever, Kent (frontispiece). Sir Thomas, as already mentioned, was the father of Anne Bullen or Boleyn, and so, during her period of favour at court, was able to amass a substantial fortune. He was also a friend of Erasmus, who stayed with him in Hever Castle. Another good brass, now badly mutilated, was that to William Porter, 1524, in Hereford Cathedral (Fig 14), the surviving parts of which are a fine representation of the Annunciation and several figures of saints. Even in these, however, the draughtsmanship is very inferior to earlier work.

There are several reasons for this decline, perhaps the chief being that the brass was a Gothic concept and was outdated by the Renaissance. The new movement demanded a life-like classical mode of representation which the old conventional brasses could not supply. Then, following the Renaissance, came the Reformation and the wholesale destruction of brasses under Henry VIII and Edward VI; and the sight of such destruction not surprisingly discouraged craftsmen from making brasses.

The fall in quality of brass-work was reflected in stone, and incised slabs of the later fifteenth and early sixteenth centuries show the same decline. The designs are the same as those on brasses, with little allowance for the different technique that stone demanded. The engraving was too shallow, and, in consequence, many sixteenth-century incised slabs have worn more than earlier, better engraved, slabs. An enormous example in the crypt of Hereford Cathedral, commemorating Andrew and Elizabeth Jones, 1497, even though it is raised up on an altar-tomb, is difficult to make out because of its shallow engraving, as well as a host of graffiti which the softer nature of stone attracted. The design, however, could never have been worth looking at since it was clumsy and crude with a top-heavy canopy.

After 1550 the design of brasses began to improve, but the quality of the metal declined. Formerly brass had been imported in sheets of up to a centimetre thick, but after the Reformation brass foundries were set up in England and, with the economic decline of the country, much thinner sheets, sometimes no more than a millimetre thick, were turned out. As a result engraving could not be so deep and the tread of passing feet was enough to wear away the lines altogether and also to loosen and crack the brass. An increasing number of engravers circumvented this danger by setting the brasses up on the wall, but even mural brasses sometimes buckled and they were always more vulnerable to deliberate damage.

RENAISSANCE REVIVAL

The decline and fall of engraved monuments, however, was not final. With more settled times in the reign of Queen Elizabeth, brass-engravers seem to have taken heart again. Repeated edicts from the Queen had prohibited the plunder of monuments in the name of religion, and increasing

*Fig 14.* William Porter, 1524 (fragments), Hereford
Cathedral

trade and prosperity brought new craftsmen, better materials and a wider
demand for brasses.

The beginnings of the revival are seen before Elizabeth's reign, about
1550, when a Renaissance style of drawing began to appear, but the art did
not begin to flourish again until the end of the century, as was shown by
the commission of a series of tombs for members of the Gage family. Four
brasses and a tomb with effigies in Firle church near Lewes, another brass

to the same family at Framfield near Uckfield, and a similar brass to the Shelleys at Clapham near Worthing, all in Sussex, were made by Gerard Johnson of Southwark between 1595 and 1600. The contract for the engraving of the Gage brasses has already been mentioned in Chapter 2, and the work of Johnson will be further discussed in the next chapter. He is important because he made the first major memorials of the Renaissance in brass. They are larger than their immediate predecessors, better engraved on stronger plates, and, above all, well designed. The medieval effigy was abandoned in favour of life-like figures drawn in the round with a lot of shading, but shading that was successful, unlike the medieval attempts. The brass had made the important step towards becoming a picture, not an icon.

The seventeenth century saw the spread of this idea. Many brasses were made on rectangular plates to emphasise their new pictorial character, and interesting background scenes began to appear. At first, as at Chichester Cathedral, 1592 or St Margaret's, Westminster, 1597, the background is merely a little classical architecture or a tiled floor, but later more complicated designs are found. At Buntingford in Hertfordshire, a vicar who

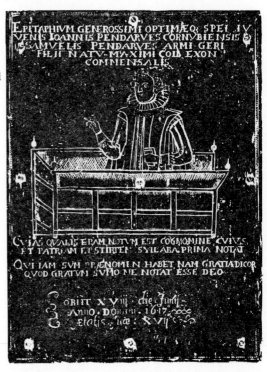

*Fig 15.* John Pendarves, 1617, St Michael's, Oxford

*Fig 16.* Anne Savage, 1606, Wormington, Gloucestershire

died in 1620 is shown in his pulpit surrounded by his congregation, while at St Michael's, Oxford, John Pendarves, a commoner of Exeter, is shown rising from his bench to speak (Fig 15). The most elaborate pictorial scenes, however, are those by Richard Haydock, already mentioned in Chapter 1. Following the style of a book-engraving, this designer produced fascinating allegorical scenes, which, quite apart from their artistic and iconographical significance, show interesting and unexpected details of everyday life. For instance, in Wells Cathedral, on the brass to Humphrey Willis, 1618, among the vanities of this world discarded by the dead man are dice and cards, a tennis racquet, a feathered hat and a pair of shoes. On the brass to Bishop Robinson at The Queen's College, Oxford, is a farm labourer holding a scythe, another a mattock and spade, a woman with a distaff and a child with a horn-book. Another Haydock brass, at St Cross Holywell, Oxford, shows a woman who died in childbirth in her two-poster bed. Several other contemporary brasses show women in bed,

*Fig 17.*   Johanna Strode, 1649, Shepton Mallet, Somerset

one of the finest being at Wormington, Gloucestershire (Fig 16). The largest
of these pictorial plates is that at Shepton Mallet, Somerset, to William
Strode and his family, dated 1649 (Fig 17): the setting is a Renaissance
church with brasses on the floor (probably the only example of brasses
within a brass) and a large tomb in the centre, on either side of which kneel
the family; from the tomb Death is rising and striking down the mother
of the family with his dart, while her husband protests in vain. Here the
brass has become so much a picture that it is actually framed and hung
on the church wall. The purpose behind the medieval brass is now ignored.

A local workman's attempt to imitate this style is shown in the touching
memorial to Thomas Tompkins of Llandinabo near Hereford, who was
drowned at an early age in 1629: he is shown in a circular pond surrounded
by bullrushes (Fig 18), and below him is a little verse in Latin:

> *Me prius infantem seruauit pura renatum,*
> *postea me puerum turbida mersit aqua*
> *Sic bis lotus eram foedus, sed nunc sine labe*
> *Ablutus Christi sanguine semper ero.*

> First did pure water wash a babe regained,
> Then muddy water drowned me immature.
> Thus was I twice washed clean, but now, unstained,
> Washed with the blood of Christ for ever more.

In addition to these rectangular plates there are still a number of cut-out figures, stylistically ranking with the pictorial brasses, but more traditional in appearance. Such are Richard Barttelot and his wives, 1614 (engraved c 1630) at Stopham in Sussex, and, the largest brass of the century, Archbishop Harsnett of Chigwell in Essex, 1631 (Figs 1, 37).

There were still, of course, bad brasses, some of the lesser brasses of the seventeenth century exemplifying all the worst characteristics of the decline. Smaller brasses became far more numerous after about 1590, probably because they had become cheaper, not being fixed in the stone at the workshop as previously, but sent out loose, to be fixed locally. This reduced the cost of transport. Most of these little brasses are to be found fixed to the wall, sometimes with screws instead of rivets. The wording is often florid and frequently in verse. The person commemorated was usually praised in extravagant and flattering terms, which sometimes make amusing reading. A typical example from Udimore, near Rye in East Sussex, runs as follows:

> Heere lyes interr'd a corps who was in life
> Heyre of John Burdet and Margret his wife,
> Coheyre of William Burdet: this hir birth,
> But much more gentle for hir genuine worth.
> In Pious, Prudent, Peaceful, Praiseful life,
> Fitting a Sarah, and a Sacred's wife,

*Fig 18.* Thomas Tompkins, 1629, Llandinabo, Herefordshire

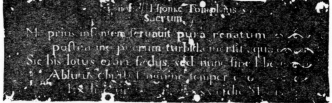

Such as John Brabon (heyre ye Pastor stil)
Whose joy of life, Death, in hir death, did kill.

(She died in holiness, in childbirth, on the 19th of October, in the year
of salvation 1626, of her age 24, in ripe time for her: too early for me.)

Thy rest gives mee a restlesse life
Becaus thou wert a matchlesse wife,
But yet I rest in Hope to see
That day of Christ, and then see thee.

(United in love and sorrow, John Brabon composed and laid this)

The revival in brasses brought with it a partial revival in incised slabs.
Two West Hampshire examples in slate—at Buriton, 1617, and Warblington,
c 1590—show kneeling figures drawn in the new manner. A more elaborate
slab at Cuckfield in Sussex shows an inscription held up by an angel and
bordered by curious and even naïve symbols illustrating various texts—'Look
up, my heart' is illustrated by a heart in which is set an eye looking upwards
(Fig 19).

Incised slabs were, however, gradually replaced by marble wall-plaques
or ledger-slabs and there are very few true incised slabs from the seventeenth century. Iron slabs, on the other hand, were popular during the late
sixteenth and seventeenth centuries, nearly all in Sussex but a few in other
iron-producing counties. The only figure I know of is at Crowhurst near
Lingfield in Surrey, showing Anne Forster, 1591, in a shroud, with her
children kneeling below (Fig 20); but there are a great number of inscriptions, some with shields, and as many as thirty can be found in the church
of Wadhurst near the Kent border. In that district iron was much cheaper
than brass. Iron was also more durable, but it was difficult to work and
could not take any fine detail. The Forster slab followed several unsuccessful castings, one of which has now been placed in East Grinstead church
and another in Ardingly. Because of the difficulty of casting, as well as the
decline in the Sussex iron industry, iron tombs died out in the beginning of
the eighteenth century. Very occasionally, as at West Hoathly, near East
Grinstead, iron slabs were used as settings for brasses, but this practice
never became common.

## THE LATEST BRASSES

The eleven years of the Commonwealth from 1649 to 1660, with the
widespread destruction of brasses, and a general disapproval of any form
of 'superstitious monument' or 'graven image', effectively brought the

*Page 49* John and Ellen Wautone, 1347, Wimbish, Essex

*Page 50* Indents of part of the Goring brass, 1558, Burton, Sussex

*Fig 19.* Incised Slab: Guy Carleton, 1628, Cuckfield, Sussex

making of figure brasses to an end. Only about twenty were laid from 1660 until the mid-nineteenth century and these are mostly very small. An exception is the interesting brass to Nicholas Toke, 1680, at Great Chart, near Ashford, Kent, who is shown in full armour with his three daughters. He had five wives, whose coats-of-arms are inlaid in white stone, and he

*Fig 20.* Cast-iron slab: Anne Forster, 1591, Crowhurst, Surrey

*Fig 21.* Nicholas Toke, 1680, Great Chart, Kent (inscription and shields omitted)

died at the age of 93 while walking to London in search of a sixth. The brass is similar in style to early seventeenth-century examples but is engraved on very thick plates (Fig 21).

Of the remaining figure brasses the best is probably the little plate to Mrs Dorothy Williams, at Pimperne near Blandford Forum in Dorset, dated 1694. Under the inscription is drawn the soul rising out of the dead skeleton. The draughtsmanship is beautiful and the brass, one of the few that are signed, is marked 'Edmund Colepeper fecit' (Fig 22). The last figures of the old tradition are two very inferior rectangular plates at St Mary Cray, South London (formerly Kent). They show Philadelphia Greenwood, 1747, and her husband, Benjamin, 1773; but they are crudely drawn and very lightly engraved.

If figure brasses died out, inscriptions were still very common, sometimes accompanied by shields, death's heads or other decorations. The wording of the inscriptions continued largely to follow that of the earlier seventeenth century, but the design of the lettering became neater and many inscriptions are beautifully engraved in 'copper-plate' script; while brasses as late or later than the Greenwood figures already mentioned are well cut and preserved.

Quite a large number of late seventeenth- and eighteenth-century inscriptions are in fact coffin-plates that have become detached from their coffins and been laid as if they were normal brasses. At Newport, Shropshire, and Malpas, south of Chester, are great collections of such plates, and

*Fig 22.* Dorothy
Williams, 1694,
Pimperne, Dorset

there are several dozen loose in the crypt of St Bride's, Fleet Street, London.

Inscriptions and coffin-plates continue right through the eighteenth century and up to about 1850 without much change. In the middle of the nineteenth century, however, while the 'Romantic Revival' was in full swing, it was inevitable that the medieval type of brass should again become popular. Two Victorian clergymen, Charles Boutell and Herbert Haines, published books on brasses, the latter including the first general list of brasses in Britain; and the interest these books aroused led to the laying of a number of brasses in the Gothic style. Many of them, in fact, dressed their figures in medieval costume, which, while tolerable for clergymen, is absurd for politicians or army officers. But some used contemporary dress and these, though rather stiff and dull in design, are not to be despised. The inscriptions, of course, had to be in the peculiar 'Gothick' script invented in the nineteenth century. Thousands of such inscriptions must have been made, since very few churches are without some, either as monuments or war memorials, recording the gift of a window or even reserving a pew.

The First World War produced a few individual brasses, notably one to an officer at Sledmore in Yorkshire dated 1915, and the brass to the Unknown Soldier in Westminster Abbey, which reverts to the earliest type with the inscription in separate letters. There are also brasses to a monk at Downside Abbey and a bishop at Ampleforth Abbey, both dated 1915. After this date, however, figure brasses died out almost completely. The latest I know of is at West Hoathly near East Grinstead, Sussex, made in 1940 to commemorate Ann Tree, who was burnt in 1556. A revival in the art of brass-making would probably depend on the inspiration of some artist who could adapt the medium to modern idioms. I can imagine that Eric Gill, if he had ever attempted it, could have produced some very interesting modern brasses.

### DESTRUCTION OF BRASSES

In the course of time many more than half the brasses laid down have been destroyed. Few losses can genuinely be attributed to accident. Brasses are very durable and can withstand a great deal of rough treatment. They survived the flames when Little Horkesley church in Essex and All Hallows Barking, London, were bombed during the Second World War, though some fierce fires have destroyed them, as apparently in Coventry and Old St Paul's Cathedrals. Wear and tear from the feet of congregations, specially when nailed boots were common, destroyed a few brasses, and must have been responsible for the loss of many of the little details of early brasses, particularly the separate letters of the first inscriptions. But the loss of more than half the brasses in England is mainly due to human carelessness or greed.

Brass was a valuable metal and easy to melt down and sell, so brasses were worth stealing. But common theft for profit was not nearly so dangerous as theft on religious or political grounds during the Reformation or the Civil War. Although Oliver Cromwell is often blamed for the destruction of brasses, more responsibility rests on Henry VIII's minister, Thomas Cromwell. When the great religious houses of England were dissolved during the sixteenth century, everything of value was stolen, including the brasses. The churches of the great abbeys must have been paved with tomb-slabs and brasses, hardly any of which survive. Only Westminster and St Albans retain any substantial number and both have been badly plundered. At Glastonbury only two letters of an inscription survive, while at the abbeys of Fountains, Tintern, Battle and many more, nothing remains but an occasional empty indent or a fragment of one. Monastic brasses were reduced from hundreds to a handful. A few were removed from churches in time, probably by relations of the deceased, and so were preserved. John Weever, in his *Discourse of Sepulchrall Monuments*, published in 1631, writes of this work of preservation: 'And likewise we cannot but love the memory of such who upon the dissolution and finall destruction of our religious structures, caused so many funerall monuments, with the bodies therin included, to bee removed into other neighbouring Churches, where by all likelihood they may rest in peace and safety untill the last sound of the Trumpet'.

Brasses that have been removed from a church are obviously difficult to identify, but a good example is the brass already mentioned in Cowfold, Sussex, to Thomas Nelond, Prior of Lewes. He is known to have been buried in Lewes Priory and so the brass must have been moved when the Priory was dissolved—no mean feat, considering that the stone is over 10 ft long and had to be carted nearly 15 miles over the Sussex Downs. Another monument from Lewes Priory, a fine carved stone originally made for Gundrada, the Foundress of the Priory, was moved up the River Ouse to Isfield and appropriated for a sixteenth-century grave. One other brass, which may have been rescued from Netley Abbey near Southampton, was found in a cottage, where it was being used as a fire-back. It is now in the possession of the Surrey Archaeological Society.

The plundering of brasses from monastic churches was serious enough, but almost as many were to be removed from parish churches during the iconoclastic reign of Edward VI, Henry VIII's successor. When the edict went out to remove images and all traces of Catholic worship from churches throughout England, the brasses suffered tremendously. Statues and paintings were of no commercial value, and, apart from the fun of knocking off heads there was no real temptation to damage them. Brasses on the other hand could be sold, and if there was official sanction for destroying them, then it was well worth while tearing them up and selling them. The official complaint was not, of course, against brasses as such, but against 'graven images' and idolatry. Brasses which depicted saints, or crucifixes, or whose inscription included a prayer for the dead, all suggested idolatry to the puritanical reformers and so, in the name of religion, this type of brass was condemned; and it was an easy matter for the unscrupulous to extend this condemnation to anything saleable. Usually the whole brass was torn up, but sometimes only the offending parts, such as Trinities, prayer scrolls, crosses or saints, were removed. Other brasses were 'reformed' by engraving over the proscribed scenes or inscriptions without actually removing anything. One of the few brasses in Ireland, that to Dean Sutton in St Patrick's Cathedral, Dublin, had a Trinity defaced by re-engraving. On other brasses the clauses in inscriptions relating to prayers for the dead, and sometimes even 'the year of Our Lord', were hatched over. The extreme is reached at Acton where Sir Robert de Bures' sword pommel has been deprived of its cross; it seems incredible that any Christian sect could object to an unadorned cross.

Queen Elizabeth I issued two edicts strictly forbidding any mutilation of monuments to the dead and ordering the immediate repair of all damage. While too late to save the majority of England's brasses, this did stop the plundering for the time being, though a certain amount of destruction continued, as is shown by Weever's rather gloomy comment: 'And nothing will be shortly left to continue the memory of the deseased to posteritie: pilfery, and the opinion some have that Tombes and their Epitaphs taste somewhat of Poperie, having already most sacrilegiously stolne, erazed and taken away, almost all the Inscriptions and Epitaphs'.

### RE-USED BRASSES

A great many stolen brasses were re-used in the late sixteenth and early seventeenth centuries, either as new brasses or as sundials or other objects requiring sheet metal. The old plates were turned over and cut up to make the new brasses, which are known as 're-used' or 'palimpsest' brasses. (The term 'palimpsest', though inappropriate, is generally used to refer to such reversed brasses. It properly applies to parchment manuscripts which have been *scraped again* (Greek *palin psestos*) to provide a clean surface for re-use.) These can often be detected since they are much thicker than contemporary Elizabethan plates. Also empty rivet-holes, or cracks following lines of engraving on the reverse are common signs of palimpsest brasses. A great number of these have been detected and taken up for examination and many of them have been replaced on hinges so that both sides are accessible. Some others are re-fixed in their stones with electrotypes of the reverse hung up near them. Doubtless many palimpsest brasses remain undiscovered, and there is room for research in this field. Probably more than half the palimpsest brasses in England have on the reverse a fragment of a foreign brass, usually Flemish; for in the Calvinist riots in Flanders great numbers of brasses were taken from the churches and sold to English brass-workers, and since most Flemish brasses were on rectangular plates they were more convenient to re-use than irregularly shaped English brasses. Some of these large foreign plates were cut into several new brasses, and distributed throughout England. One example is at Northiam near Rye in Sussex, where an inscription dated 1583 has, on the reverse, part of the border inscription of a Flemish brass of the early fifteenth century; a few words of the inscription and two grotesque figures survive (Fig 23). Part of the same brass is on the reverse of the figure of the wife of Edmund Eyre, dated 1563 but engraved in 1581, at Burnham, near Slough, Buckinghamshire.

Another, much rarer, form of palimpsest was made by 'appropriating' a whole figure and adding a new inscription and shields. These are easily recognisable since the costume of the figure is not contemporary with the

*Fig 23.* John Sharp, palimpsest, 1583 and c 1450, Northiam,
Sussex

date of the inscription. Sometimes an attempt has been made to bring the
figure up-to-date by filing down and re-engraving parts of it. A striking
example, at Waterperry in Oxfordshire, is a brass to Walter Curson and
his wife, c 1540, which has been made up out of the brass to Simon Kamp
and his wife, dated 1442. The male figure has been partly re-engraved and
a new head added to bring the armour up-to-date; the lower half of the
wife has hardly been changed but the upper part and the inscription were
turned over and re-engraved. Not all palimpsest brasses, however, were
plundered from other churches. Some were 'workshop wasters', ie unfinished
or rejected brasses that were never laid and were re-used by the same
workshop. These occur, of course, before the Reformation, and usually both
sides are of approximately the same date. A few examples have been found

of trial or practice engravings—maybe an apprentice learning the feel of the medium by doodling on the back of a plate.

### REVOLUTION AND RESTORATION

The royal edicts mentioned above ordered the full restoration of all damage done to tombs and monuments, but very little repair work was in fact done. One example of Elizabethan restoration is at Minster-in-Sheppey, Kent, where the figure of a knight, c 1330, who had lost his legs had them replaced with a palimpsest fragment; but at the same time a strip was cut out of the original figure to make him the same height as the lady of approximately the same date who was supposed to be his wife. The strip was restored in 1881, leaving the brass a combination of three different dates (Fig 72). Other restorations, of the early seventeenth century, were carried out by descendants of the families commemorated on the brasses, as at Stopham near Pulborough in Sussex, and Pluckley near Ashford in Kent. These brasses were rather clumsily restored, those at Pluckley in a bad imitation of the original style, and those at Stopham by the addition of figures dressed in costume of the Charles I period.

Even while these restorations were being carried out, and while the revival of brass-engraving already described was in full swing, the far sighted could foresee yet another period of widespread destruction. Archbishop Harsnett ordered his brass to be laid in the remote parish church where he had first been vicar rather than in his cathedral; he also made it an inch thick and had it riveted right through the stone, so that it was almost impossible to move. Thus it escaped the holocaust at York. The Civil War brought more spectacular destruction of brasses, though this was confined almost entirely to the great cathedrals and was never as widespread as the sixteenth-century devastation. The loss to the cathedrals, however, was almost total, since every scrap of metal was needed for munitions. In two afternoons Cromwell and his men stripped York and Lincoln Minsters of over 200 brasses each. Not a scrap of brass remains in most of the greater cathedrals of England and the cream of English brass-work was lost for ever. Nor was the Royal party blameless: most of Oxford Cathedral's brasses were melted into gunshot by Charles I. By the time of the Restoration brasses were reduced to the few that had escaped by the chance of being in out-of-the-way country churches, though even these had suffered, since in the church-warden's accounts for 1644 in Walberswick, Suffolk, is this significant entry: 'Received for 40lbs. of brass from out of ye church, for which Niefe the glasher of Sould [Southwold] offered 3d. ob. ye li ............ 11s 8d'.

Since then there has been no organised destruction of brasses but one by one they have continued to disappear. The clergy, who were supposedly responsible for the churches and their contents, often showed little consideration for the memorials of the dead. At King's Lynn in Norfolk an enormous Flemish brass was sold in the eighteenth century by the sexton, who afterwards hanged himself in the belfry. As I have already described, much of the brass of St Thomas of Hereford was picked out by the choirboys.

The worst of all, however, were the so-called 'restorers' who devastated most of our churches in the late nineteenth century. Many brasses were simply thrown away during 'restorations', others sold, others buried under new flooring. Even those that were preserved were often torn up from their slabs and left loose in the church chest, where many still lie, or were nailed to a wall, often with the pieces of brass in the wrong positions. Two figures, at Calbourne in the Isle of Wight and Wilburton near Ely, were set horizontally on the wall. In Hereford Cathedral most of the brasses were quite arbitarily mixed up and stuck on the walls; this has largely been put right, but one or two pieces are still upside down. Other brasses were set up so high that one can hardly see them, as at St Mary the Virgin, Oxford; while others were hidden behind organs, as at Corpus Christi College, Oxford. A few, which were allowed to remain in their original slabs, were given inscriptions of completely different date, as at Horley, Surrey, where an inscription of 1516 has been fitted on to a figure of c 1420. Yet other brasses were covered with glass, which, of course, reflects light and makes the brass very difficult to see, as at Newcastle-on-Tyne. Some brasses were 'filled in' with some black substance, which, after a few years' accumulated dirt, made the entire brass uniformly black and obscured the design, as at Pulborough, Sussex. Others that escaped all this 'restoring' were relaid in new slabs that omitted the outlines of the missing parts, sometimes leaving the design quite puzzling, as at Ashford, Kent (Figs 12, 13). The final assault on brasses was made, and far too often is still being made, by polishing them vigorously with artificial polish, which soon makes them appear as worn and featureless as an old lawyer's doorplate.

With such lack of consideration for existing brasses, it is not surprising that indents were treated with even less care: the majority were cut up or filled with cement, buried under tiles or laid as churchyard paths, and with their destruction went the only record of many lost brasses. This period of vandalism, however, was countered by a rise of interest in brasses and the formation in 1887 of the Monumental Brass Society, which has recently done a great deal to repair the damage of the Victorian age. The twentieth century has seen a more reasonable approach to brasses and general conservation has become the rule. Fortunately, the metal is no longer of commercial value; yet losses still occur, small parts being picked out to satisfy the souvenir hunter. Even the church authorities still shirk their responsibilities. One interesting brass 'came loose' in May 1968, and was put aside by the rector to be re-fixed by the diocesan workmen; by December the brass had been roughly fixed down, not even level with the inscription which had never come out, and an important part was completely covered with cement. Other rectors in recent years, jealous of brass-rubbers, have covered brasses with plastic, in one case apparently poured on as liquid, thus ruining the brass. Damage and maltreatment continue even today.

### PRESENT DISTRIBUTION OF BRASSES

In the face of all these waves of destruction it is remarkable how many brasses survive in England—over 8,000, far more than in any other country. The destruction of brasses was indiscriminate, so the proportions of the different types of brasses left, though not the numbers, remain about the same as when they were laid down.

In the Middle Ages all brass had to be imported, engraved, set into its stone in the workshop, and transported to the church it was destined for. Transport generally made up the bulk of the cost, and, as it varied little with the size of the brass, most stones being full size even if there was only a little inscription, all brasses became progressively more expensive the further they got from their makers. The workshops were in large cities near the east coast to which brass from Germany was imported, and so, many more brasses are found in the eastern areas, specially around London, than in the rest of England. Those further afield tended to be near main communication routes, especially navigable rivers and canals. Only the richest could afford brasses in remote areas during the Middle Ages.

The sixteenth century saw an important change, brought about not only by the development of English brass foundries, which set up new centres of distribution, but much more by the increasing practice of making small mural brasses, mostly inscriptions, which could be sent out from a workshop without a stone backing to be fixed up by the local craftsmen. A small plate of brass cost little in transport and could be put in a church almost anywhere. Seventeenth- and eighteenth-century inscriptions are far more widely distributed than any kinds of medieval brass.

Here is an analysis of the different types of brass and dates for two greatly contrasting counties—Herefordshire and Kent (excluding that part of Kent now in the London area). I am not counting the great number of nineteenth- and twentieth-century inscriptions, which have never been listed.

Kent contains 740 brasses as opposed to 72 in Herefordshire. Of these about half—383 in Kent and 31 in Herefordshire—include figures, crosses, canopies or symbolic representations such as saints, the rest being inscriptions, with or without coats-of-arms. The distribution in the two counties over the centuries is strikingly similar, beginning with a few in the early fourteenth, rising to a peak about 1600 and gradually fading out in the eighteenth century. The growth in numbers is specially noticeable in Herefordshire: from 1550 to 1600 there are only two figures and one inscription, while from 1600 to 1650 there are seven figures and sixteen inscriptions, an increase due to the number of small mural brasses mentioned above.

In the earlier centuries Kent is disproportionately well endowed since it was a rich agricultural and trading county with good communications and near the main brass-workshops in London. There was also a Kentish school of brass-makers, probably based in Canterbury; and some brasses, such as the pair at Minster-in-Sheppey, were imported, probably from France. Herefordshire, on the other hand, was an unsettled border county, a long way from London and the brass-workshops. Communications were difficult and mostly dependent on water transport. So nearly all the Herefordshire brasses occur within a few miles of the River Wye, and of the thirty-two brasses before 1600, twenty-four are in Hereford Cathedral. Herefordshire also differs from Kent in having a hard local stone suitable for making incised slabs, of which many survive. These could be made easily and cheaply on the spot and thus there was less demand for brasses.

Another factor for consideration is the extent of destruction in the two counties. Hereford saw little fighting in the Civil War and there was no plundering on the scale of Lincoln or York. Very little damage was done at all in the county, except that the Cathedral suffered greatly under 'restorers', specially after the fall of the west tower, which destroyed the nave in 1786. It still, however, contains more brass than any other English Cathedral. A few churches contain indents but there has been very little loss from the county as a whole.

Kent, on the other hand, has suffered greatly: both Canterbury and Rochester cathedrals were entirely stripped. The floor of the Martyrdom in Canterbury shows the indents of a series of really magnificent brasses and the crypt of Rochester contains several fine indents. The parish churches also were badly plundered. A typical Kentish church, Cranbrook, retains ten rather undistinguished brasses, only two of them with figures. Two others have lost their figures, while only indents remain of a further nine figure brasses and six inscriptions, three of the slabs being very early. Few churches preserved their slabs as well as Cranbrook and the total losses for Kent must have been enormous.

Bearing in mind all these factors, as well as the fact that Kent is about twice the size of Herefordshire, the numbers of brasses remaining are very different but the proportions of brass types are remarkably similar. This table gives the numbers of brasses as listed in Mill Stevenson's *List*, the most complete published. A few others are added from notes in *Monumental Brass Society Transactions*, and there are doubtless a few unlisted, but basically the figures are accurate.

| KENT | | HEREFORDSHIRE | | |
| --- | --- | --- | --- | --- |
| FIGURES | INSCRIPTIONS | FIGURES | INSCRIPTIONS | DATES |
| 27 | 5 | 4 | 0 | 1282–1400 |
| 69 | 20 | 5 | 2 | 1401–1450 |
| 74 | 29 | 8 | 3 | 1451–1500 |
| 109 | 31 | 5 | 2 | 1501–1550 |
| 58 | 99 | 2 | 1 | 1551–1600 |
| 44 | 127 | 7 | 16 | 1601–1650 |
| 2 | 22 | 0 | 11 | 1651–1700 |
| 0 | 24 | 0 | 6 | 1701–1800 |
| 383 | 357 | 31 | 41 | TOTALS |

It must not, of course, be assumed that figure brasses necessarily identify the rich and important, and inscriptions the poor and humble: often noblemen or bishops were content with a short inscription, while lesser but more ostentatious people sought immortality in large and expensive brasses. A great many simple inscriptions, however, particularly in the sixteenth century and after, were undoubtedly to humble folk.

The two counties analysed are extreme cases, most English counties falling somewhere between the two. As I have said, brasses are thickest round London and up the east coast, the numbers gradually falling off towards the north and west. The border counties are very poor in brasses, Northumberland having no more than a single figure, and that imported from Flanders. Wales has a scattering of brasses, mostly fairly late and none of them distinguished, while Scotland has only a handful surviving, the finest being a Flemish rectangular plate in Aberdeen. Many other Flemish brasses in Scotland were destroyed at the time of John Knox in the sixteenth century. In Ireland there are five brasses in Dublin and one in County Cork, all to members of the English ruling class. There are also three inscriptions in the Isle of Man.

The distribution of brasses, therefore, depends on the prosperity and accessibility of an area. A small brass in Ireland probably cost far more than a large and elaborate brass in London. If stone suitable for making incised slabs was available in a remote area, then there were fewer brasses and more incised slabs anyway—as in Herefordshire, Cornwall and Scotland. If, as in Lincolnshire, good stone coincided with easy trade-routes, then the county was specially rich in both stone and brass. It was Oliver Cromwell's disastrous visit to Lincoln Minster that prevented Lincolnshire from being one of the richest and most interesting areas for incised memorials. Boston church alone contains twenty-five figures, inscriptions or fragments in brass; twenty incised slabs that had some parts inlaid in brass; five normal incised slabs; and sixty-one indents of brasses. When we remember that the total number of brasses plundered from Lincoln Minster is estimated at 2–700 it is clear that the number in the county must have been enormous.

Incised slabs, as I have said, are found mostly in districts with a suitable stone, particularly along the belt of liass running from Lincolnshire to Cornwall. They are particularly numerous in Leicestershire and Rutland, and to a lesser extent in Derbyshire and Gloucestershire. Isolated examples occur all over England, some from Hampshire, Sussex and Kent having already been mentioned. There are just a few in East Anglia and some good ones in Yorkshire. Most of these isolated slabs are made of imported stone, usually slate.

A sub-division of incised slabs is formed by *ledger-slabs*. These are large and usually black, with incised inscriptions and coats-of-arms, which are found in large numbers on the floors of churches all over England. A few, as at Stanmer, near Brighton, have brass coats-of-arms let in over the inscription in the stone. Many of them are beautifully cut, with elaborate decoration on the arms and good lettering. They run from the beginning of the eighteenth century to the mid-nineteenth, but they are not normally counted as incised slabs.

Victorian and modern brasses, of course, can be found everywhere in the British Isles, and commemorate all classes of society. Nor are they confined to old Anglican churches, but are found in Nonconformist chapels and Catholic churches.

Many brasses are now to be found in museums or in private possession. Some of these come from destroyed churches, but many are known to belong to certain churches and some individual brasses are known to be split between the church and a museum. It is a pity that the example of the Bodleian Library at Oxford has not been more followed, and the brasses returned to their rightful places.

# 4 ✤ The Design of Brasses

A S WORKS OF art, brasses have had little mention in books on medieval and Renaissance art and design. This is unfair, for brasses are not just historical records and ancient monuments but form an important branch of art.

## GOTHIC BRASSES

The 'Gothic' brass, unfortunately, came late in the era of Gothic art and design and its history is one of rapid decay. The first brasses appeared in the thirteenth century when the major works of Gothic architecture were already built and the Renaissance was stirring in southern Europe. Enough vigour remained, however, for the Gothic brasses to enjoy a period of splendour before collapsing with the arrival of the Renaissance in England.

As already explained, the first brasses were modelled on solid effigies of stone or wood, which were designed to show a compromise between life and death, the sleep of the faithful waiting for the Resurrection. The figures lie on their backs—the hands joined in prayer, the eyes open but unseeing. The head is raised on a helmet or pillow to prevent it from falling back, and the feet are placed against an animal, usually a lion or hound, to round off the figure (page 152).

This form of effigy, which prevailed from the beginning of the Middle Ages until the mid-sixteenth century, was disturbed in the late thirteenth century by a new movement—one of vitality and unrest—which happened to coincide with the earliest brasses. Thus, with the exception of Sir John Daubernoun, 1277, all the first brasses show this new style and it is not until about 1370 that the stiff effigy style appears again in brasses, just as it returned in stone. A typical example of this stiff style is Sir William de Bryene, 1395, from Seal, near Sevenoaks, Kent (title page). Here the essential lines of the design are shown in bold strokes of the burin, and the features of an effigy faithfully reproduced.

The movement towards vitality in the late thirteenth century, inspired

*Fig 24.* John de Mereworth, 1366, Mereworth, Kent

probably by the first rumblings of the Italian Renaissance, was at first expressed in crossing the legs of the figures whether they were crusaders or not. It was a more comfortable way of lying and showed rather more alertness than the former effigies. Stone effigies, indeed, are often shown rolling over, one hand grasping the sword hilt, as if on the point of rising to fight. Brasses are more restrained: though the legs are crossed the hands are still joined in prayer, the faces still calm and impassive. The finest of these figures is the knight at Acton, Suffolk (Fig 8).

The next development in posture is shown well on the brasses at Elsing, Norfolk, and Wimbish, Essex, both 1347 (Fig 31; page 49). On these the figures are twisted into an S-curve, an alert but uncomfortable position. This posture appears also on stained-glass, in painting and carving, and was widespread for a short period. The side figures on the Elsing brass have close parallels in stained-glass, and the figures at the top, representing the Coronation of the Virgin, are almost identical to those on the Pienza Cope, a typical specimen of English (probably East Anglian) needlework (page 133).

Other brasses of the mid-thirteenth century have a less accentuated twist, hardly noticeable at Westley Waterless near Newmarket, 1325 and Stoke D'Abernon, Surrey, 1327 (Fig 30), but quite comical at Cobham, c 1367, and Mereworth, 1366, both in Kent (Figs 32, 24). By 1370 figures are quite straight and rigid again, the only exceptions being a few couples shown hand in hand, as at Trotton, Sussex, 1419 (Fig 34).

Brasses other than armoured figures follow more or less the same pattern of development, even to the crossed legs, which are suggested by the lines of the drapery of Margarete de Camoys, c 1310 at Trotton, Sussex (Fig 9). An exception was the small figure of a lady recently stolen from Sedgefield, Durham, c 1310, which was kneeling. Half-effigies had no special style of their own but were drawn merely as truncated full-length figures, broken off sometimes at the waist, sometimes along the bottom line of the arms.

The designers of the earliest brasses remain anonymous: they never signed their names and the only clues they left were tricks of style, which can be detected on different brasses. The medieval artist's name was considered irrelevant—the art was considered more important than the artist. A possible maker's mark can be seen stamped on the brass at Westley Waterless, which shows a reversed N, a mallet, star and crescent. The same device, without the letter N, appears also on the seal of a deed dated 1277, with the name Walter le Masun, and may possibly be the mark of some guild of masons. If so it provides interesting evidence of the link between stone- and brass-work. Two other brasses have marks that may possibly be connected with the Westley Waterless mark: a crescent at Chartham, Kent, 1306 and a reversed N at Trotton, Sussex, 1419. If these are related they can only signify a guild of workmen, since both date and style prove that these brasses are not by the same hand.

After about 1350 there are enough surviving brasses to enable one to pick out a number of 'schools of engraving', some of which remained in operation right through the fifteenth century. Each is distinguished by certain details, such as the shape of the nose, and the design of little pieces of armour such as knee-caps. All military effigies between 1360 and 1485 have been classified and allotted to one or other of these schools in an

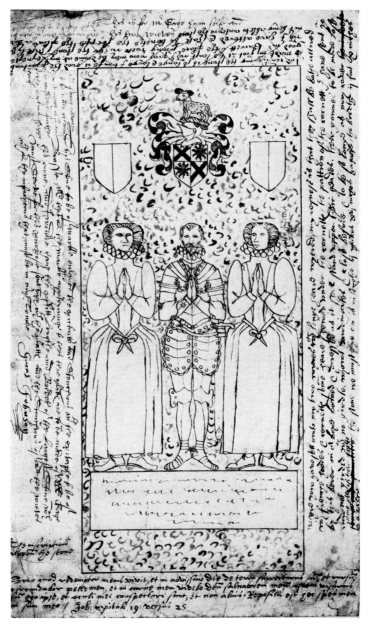

*Page 67* Sketch by Gerard Johnson for brass to John Gage and wives,
1595, Firle House, Sussex

*Page 68* Monument to John Donne, 1631, St Paul's Cathedral, London;
illustration from W. Dugdale's *History of St Paul's*, 1716

excellent article by J. P. C. Kent (in the *Journal of the British Archaeological Association* for 1949), who traces the stylistic development in minute detail and is thus able to re-date many brasses on these grounds alone.

The first great school, identified as 'Series A', begins with a notable collection of six knights dated between 1365 and 1368: these are the three at Cobham, Kent, all probably engraved c 1367 (Fig 32), though the men commemorated died in 1354, 1367 and 1408 respectively; one near by at Mereworth, 1366 (Fig 24); one at Drayton Beauchamp near Aylesbury, Buckinghamshire, 1368; and one at Freshwater, Isle of Wight, c 1365. Although these are all so similar in style that there can be no doubt that they are by the same hand, yet each is distinguished in some way: one of the knights at Cobham holds a model of the church, the Drayton Beauchamp figure has bells hanging on his knees and the Freshwater knight has a shield on the front of his armour.

By the end of the fourteenth century the main schools were established; the brass-engravers had matured and become conventional. Inevitably this led to many dull brasses, though some fine and original work still appeared. It is often difficult to distinguish between the different schools of engraving at this time, though each still kept some of its individual characteristics.

The development of canopies on brasses closely followed the development of architecture, and as the Decorated style evolved into the Perpendicular, so the canopies increased in height and magnificence. The earliest canopies centred the gables on the forehead of the figure, but by the end of the fourteenth century the centres were a long way above the head. All through the century, however, a due proportion was kept and the canopies were designed on the Golden Section, in which the ratio of the height of the gable to the height of the shafts is as the height of the shafts to the total height.

At first the canopies had very little engraved detail, being cut out and pierced wherever possible; but this made them fragile and so after about 1350 the details came increasingly to be engraved on unified plates. More and more complicated designs were evolved as the simplicity of the Decorated style gave place to the elaborate decoration of the Perpendicular.

In addition to flat brass memorials the fourteenth century evolved brass three-dimensional monuments. The amount of metal needed was so great that its cost prevented any but royalty and their close followers from having such monuments, but the few examples remaining are among the most splendid tombs in England. Nearly all of them are in Westminster Abbey, where also lies the effigy of Sir William de Valence, 1296, father of those commemorated by the two earliest brass inscriptions (see p 33). His figure is made of wood entirely plated with sheets of brass, on which details such

E

as chain-mail are engraved. The surface was originally gilded and in part enamelled (page 134). This figure is clearly related to the great royal tombs, which are cast in brass and gilded. The earliest is that of Henry III and Eleanor of Castile, made about 1291 by William Torel, goldsmith of London. On the back of the large plate on which the effigies rest are engraved some figures in the same style as normal brasses, showing that Torel probably made flat brasses as well as cast effigies. Another craftsman who worked in cast brass was John Orchard, who made the tombs of Edward III in Westminster Abbey and the Black Prince in Canterbury Cathedral. Edward III's tomb is one of the earliest to show children, who are represented by little brass figures on its sides, with their coats-of-arms enamelled on flat plates of brass (page 151).

The most magnificent of the royal tombs in brass is that of Richard II and Anne of Bohemia, made between 1394 and 1397 by Nicholas Broker and Godfrey Prest, citizens and coppersmiths of London. These two again almost certainly made flat brasses, though no record remains of such work.

During the fifteenth century the Gothic genius burnt itself out until, by the Tudor period, its art was virtually dead. Brasses proliferated—there are probably more fifteenth-century figures than those of any other century —but the standard of design decayed. In the first half of the century brasses remained competent but monotonous and the existing workshops increased their production considerably.

The largest and most widespread of these workshops was that classified as 'Series B', whose work is distinguishable by the unusual outline of the face, with a square chin, and the frequent use of a little four-petalled rose with elongated sepals. Examples of almost every class in English society can be found, such as a knight and his wife at Yoxford, Suffolk, 1428; a lady at Hellingly, Sussex, c 1440; a civilian at Northleach, Gloucestershire, 1458; a priest at Horsham, Sussex, 1427 (Fig 45); a monk at St Albans Abbey, c 1460 (Fig 46); an abbot from the same abbey, 1451; a shroud at Taplow, Buckinghamshire, 1455 (Fig 52); an academic in Merton College Chapel, Oxford, 1445; and a judge and his wife at Graveney, Kent, 1436. Although no two are identical, there is no variety in posture or quality of line. The drawing is skilful and economic but it has lost the majesty of that of the great fourteenth-century brasses. This workshop must have enjoyed some prestige, for it had imitators whose workmen, though very inferior, obviously copied the designs, as in a small half-effigy of a priest now in Worthing Museum, Sussex.

The workshop of 'Series D' produced a group of brasses rather like those of 'Series B', fewer in number but superior in quality, during the fifteenth century. Its distinguishing badge is a little five-petalled rose repeated along the flat tops of canopies at Arundel, Sussex, 1430; Lingfield, Surrey, 1420 (Fig 79); Trotton, Sussex, 1419 (Fig 34); and Constance Cathedral, Germany, on the English brass to Robert Hallum, Bishop of Salisbury, 1417. This rose also appears on the shoulder-roundels of the armour at Trotton and at Thame, Oxfordshire, c 1420. Another feature of these 'Series D' brasses is a beautiful 'rose window' in the centre of the gables on the canopies at Trotton and Arundel and also at Broadwater near Worthing, Sussex, 1432.

After about 1480 schools of engraving proliferated and there are no longer definite series. The old designs lapsed. There is little work of any distinction, though a few unusual brasses attract attention. The old effigy style was gradually superseded by more realistic representations, either shrouded figures or skeletons which are gruesomely dead, or normal figures alive and standing on a grassy mound. Many of these standing figures, however, still have their heads resting on a helmet or cushion. Children were now usually shown on their parents' brasses, often in little groups under the main figures but occasionally as diminutive figures next to or in front of them. Praying with the hands outstretched, rare before on brasses, became increasingly common.

Draughtsmanship declined visibly from the mid-fifteenth century onwards as greater attempts in realism forced the designers into a style beyond their ability. More lines were used and shading added, often quite arbitrarily without paying any attention to the supposed source of light. The result was strained postures, grotesque faces and rigid drapery. The designers also tried to get the canopies into perspective, but only succeeded in making them appear precarious and clumsy; while the pinnacles were carried too high and the proportion of shaft to pinnacle lost. The concept of the recumbent effigy finally came to an end with the development of a style of lady's headdress that could only be appreciated in profile; figures consequently were turned half-face, and all semblance of repose lost.

Towards the end of the century a number of regional schools of engraving sprang up, each with certain characteristics. Yorkshire brasses tend to be rather elongated; East Anglian work is naïve but well executed, and its workmen turned out a number of chalices as memorials to priests; Midland brasses are based on London styles, but are less skilful and show inferior draughtsmanship; and more remote areas such as Cornwall are typified by very rough local work, poor imitations of brasses from London.

An important London school produced a number of brasses to ecclesiastics, identifiable by wide orphreys of unusual design, as if studded with jewels. A mitre on the tomb of Bishop Russell, 1494, the only surviving brass in Lincoln Minster, shows these 'jewels' filled with coloured enamels. Similar orphreys survive at Higham Ferrers, Northamptonshire, usually

Fig 25. Bishop John Bowthe, 1478, East Horsley, Surrey

dated 1523 but almost certainly engraved earlier; Westminster Abbey, 1498; East Horsley near Guildford, 1478 (Fig 25); and Faversham, Kent, 1480.

The Renaissance came to England in the early years of the sixteenth century when Pietro Torrigiano arrived to build a tomb for Henry VII. English painters, sculptors and architects soon absorbed the new ideas from immigrant artists and, though a certain amount of Gothic lingered on, the classical revival was soon under way. Brasses, however, remained unchanged and continued to decay on Gothic lines until the reign of Queen Elizabeth. Early sixteenth-century brasses are marked by an increased use of religious symbols, figures of saints and scriptural scenes, all rather badly designed. When the Reformation forbade such designs the craftsmen were left practically without subjects. Brilliant colouring and heraldic ostentation attempted to cover up the deficiencies of design, but these brasses are seldom more than vulgar. Exceptions are a few brasses to specially rich men, such as Sir Thomas Bullen (frontispiece).

The only original feature in the early sixteenth century was the increasing use of mural brasses, presumably because the floors of many churches were already fully occupied. A common design for these murals was a pair of kneeling figures under some religious device, usually the Trinity. Many of this type have been despoiled of their Trinities, but the figures and inscriptions survive. The children are now frequently shown kneeling behind their parents. These brasses were usually heraldic and their mural position has protected many of them well enough for the colouring to remain. After the mural paintings in the churches were destroyed or painted over, the whole wall space was made available for monuments and the usual position for a brass from about 1540 onwards was on the wall.

There were no prominent schools of engraving in the early sixteenth century but the local workshops continued to produce much the same sort of brass as they had in the late fifteenth century. After the Reformation a few workshops seem to have made a speciality of re-using old brasses, and these are worth tracing for the sake of what is on the reverse. A good series of such brasses from one particular workshop has been traced to Easton Neston near Towcester, 1552, and Charwelton near Daventry, 1541 (Fig 57), both in Northamptonshire; Somerton in Oxfordshire, 1552; and Ludford, Herefordshire, 1554, which brass is still unexamined on its reverse side.

CLASSICAL BRASSES

Just as Torrigiano and Holbein were needed to bring the Renaissance into English sculpture and English painting, so it was a foreigner, Geraert Janssen who brought English brasses, last of all the arts, into the neo-classical fold. Born in Amsterdam, he arrived in England about 1567, when he changed his name to Gerard Johnson; but he did not become active as a designer until about 1595. In that year he received a commission from John Gage of Firle Place, near Lewes, Sussex, for a series of five tombs for various members of the Gage family. The correspondence relating to this commission has already been mentioned (p 21). Johnson built two altar-tombs against the wall of Firle church, with an arch above them, let into the wall, the brass figures lying on the tombs, and the shields and inscription fixed on the wall under the arch. On the side of the tomb-chests are further inscriptions cut in alabaster. The third and largest of the tombs, for Sir John Gage KG and his wife, has a similar tomb-chest, but standing out from the wall, with recumbent effigies in alabaster and an inscription with shields in brass. The settings for the remaining brasses are lost, and the figures are now set in new stones on the wall. The basic elements of these tombs are Gothic, but all the detail is correctly Renaissance, so the tombs do not clash either with the Gothic church or with their Renaissance contemporaries. The figures are drawn as vividly and as realistically as is possible in such a medium. For the first time shading is used successfully, giving roundness to the figures (Fig 3, and page 67).

Other brasses identifiable as Johnson's work can be seen at Framfield and Clapham in Sussex—two very similar mural rectangular plates with kneeling figures on either side of a prayer-desk (Fig 59)—and at Upton near Slough, Buckinghamshire, 1599—a man in armour with his wife. Here the wife is dressed in the costume Johnson had designed for the ladies at Firle, but which John Gage had insisted on altering. Several other brasses have been ascribed to Johnson and about fifty carved stone monuments are attributed to him or his sons.

Johnson was the first of a number of individual craftsmen who produced the finest brasses of the Renaissance. Portraits superseded effigies and so designs became more original. Far more is known about the designers of the Renaissance period than the medieval.

One of its leaders was Richard Haydock, a physician, and fellow of New College, Oxford. Although sharing his name with several eminent Catholic counter-Reformationists, he did not share their views, for it is recorded that he 'used to see visions in the night; that he would select a text in his sleep, and discourse on it in spite of pinchings, generally denouncing the Pope and high church practices' (Wilson's *History of Great Britain*, 1653). This familiarity with texts is evident in his work—scriptural quotations are inserted in every possible position in his brasses. These are all small rectangular plates, crammed with detail that looks more like etching than engraving, and can be found at Oxford in New College Chapel, 1623, St Cross Holywell, 1622 and The Queen's College, two of 1616; Wells Cathedral, 1618; and Tingewick near Buckingham, 1608. Two others formerly in New College are now lost. All have allegorical designs and texts. Their attitude to the composition of the memorial is completely new: the brass to Bishop Robinson in Queen's is the most elaborate and will serve as an example to be examined in detail (Fig 26). The Bishop, dressed in strict Low Church manner, is kneeling in front of his two cares, Carlisle Cathedral and The Queen's College. His flock is represented both symbolically, by sheep herded into wattle sheepfolds and guarded by Welsh border collies, and realistically, by a group of countrymen with their farm instruments, a woman with a distaff and a child holding up her horn-book, inscribed 'ABC'. The Bishop holds a candle with the Greek text 'To enlighten them that sit in darkness', which is continued in Latin under the feet of the countrymen: 'to direct our feet into the way of peace' (*Luke*, i, 79). Before the Bishop is a pile of broken weapons with, in Latin, 'They shall turn their swords into plough shares and their spears into sickles' (*Isiah*, ii, 4) and, in English, 'Deadly Feude extinte' with the reference to *Isiah*, xi, 6 'The wolf shall dwell with the lamb', suitably illustrated. At the top of the plate the heavens open and an angel flies out with two scrolls, one in Latin 'And there were in the same country shepherds watching and

*Fig 26.* Bishop Henry Robinson, 1616, The Queen's College,
Oxford

keeping the night-watches over their flock' (*Luke*, ii, 8), and in Greek, 'To
the watchers' or 'bishops'. All this refers obviously to the Bishop's function
as shepherd, looking after and guiding his flock, and the point is
emphasised also by the inscription along his crozier identifying the various
parts—the point for correcting, the staff to lean on, and the crook to catch
and guide, while an eye and a crane stand for vigilance. There is a duplicate
of this brass in Carlisle Cathedral.

Another artist who made great use of allegory was Epiphany Evesham, a sculptor who worked chiefly on large stone monuments, such as one at Lynsted near Sittingbourne, Kent, which he signed. The only surviving brass signed by him is at Marsworth, Buckinghamshire, near Tring, dated 1618, which shows a man reclining on top of a tomb, with his family kneeling round him, and Death appearing from behind a curtain, brandishing a dart. This brass is placed on one end of an altar-tomb on whose sides are incised stone panels with various emblems and allegorical figures. The emblems are matched exactly on an incised slab at Cuckfield, Sussex, 1628 (Fig 19), so there can be no doubt that this is Evesham's work, which is marked not only by curious symbols but also by individual and sympathetic treatment of each figure. Horace Walpole quotes a sixteenth-century editor of Owen's *Epigrams*, mentioning Evesham: 'give me leave to insert his [Owen's] Epitaph, which is Engraved in a plate of Brasse and fixed under his Monumental Image: formed and erected by the most exquisite Artist Mr Epiphanius Evesham, within the Cathedral Church of St Paul'. Owen's brass was, of course, destroyed when the old cathedral was burnt down in 1666.

The only monument to survive from Old St Paul's is also connected with the design of brasses. The monument is the striking figure of John Donne, carved by Nicholas Stone from a painting, made just before the poet's death, for which he posed in his shroud (page 68). In 1638, seven years after Donne's death, Mary Howard, a distant relation of the Duke of Norfolk, was commemorated by a brass so closely resembling the statue of Donne (Fig 69) that it must have been copied from it, but there is no way of telling whether Nicholas Stone himself made the brass or whether it was copied by an admirer. Stone was responsible for a large number of carved monuments, though no others show shrouded figures, which by this time were very rare, and is known to have made several other brasses.

The last great name among pre-Cromwellian brass designers is Edward Marshall, also a stone carver, who signed the large rectangular brass of the Filmers at East Sutton near Maidstone, Kent, 1629. The main figures and the children underneath are lively and individual, and are almost certainly portraits. It has been suggested that the great brass of Archbishop Harsnett, 1631 (Fig 1) is also by Marshall, but there is not enough evidence to say for certain; there is some resemblance in details such as the treatment of the face, but the designs of the two brasses are very different. Harsnett's brass is almost Mannerist with its extraordinary eagle eyes, the cope bunched up, the posture full of suppressed energy as if the Archbishop were about to burst out into one of his fiery sermons. It is reminiscent of Cellini's bust of Cosimo I of Florence in its alertness and vitality.

Many other brasses of the early seventeenth century are of a very high standard and comparable with those already described, particularly the large plate at Shepton Mallet (Fig 17). Other brasses, however, are very inferior, some still clinging to the Gothic tradition, others merely incompetent attempts at the classical style. The majority of brasses at this time are inscriptions without figures, most of which, while fascinating to read, are of no artistic interest.

After the Civil War figure brasses became practically extinct, and only one is artistically important, the Baroque monument of Mrs Williams at Pimperne, Dorset, 1694 (Fig 22), signed by Edmund Colepeper, about whom nothing is known. It is a well executed design with good lettering and an interesting flow in the figure. Nearly all the other late figure brasses are rather amateurish, some being quite crude.

In contrast the engraving of inscriptions improved markedly and some of the lettering on late seventeenth- and early eighteenth-century inscriptions is beautiful, whether Roman capitals or 'copper-plate' flowing script. Small details such as skulls, hourglasses, palm branches and cherubs are also attractively drawn. Several of these brasses are signed, particularly in the North of England, where Thomas Ainsworth and the brothers Thomas and Joshua Mann were active. The last inscriptions in the classical tradition survived in remote areas well into the nineteenth century with much the same styles of lettering, though there are few important classical brasses after 1700.

REVIVALIST AND MODERN BRASSES

At the end of the eighteenth century a Gothic brass was made for a friend of Horace Walpole, and subsequent years saw a Gothic Revival in brasses, which, however, did not reach any importance until the middle of the nineteenth century. From then until the First World War, hundreds of brasses were laid, mostly inscriptions but a great many figures, too. They are nearly all of medieval inspiration, copying the late fourteenth-century styles and equipped with the full fantasy of 'Gothic lettering'. Some, like that of General Wilson, 1849, in Westminster Abbey, are merely pastiches of medieval work, showing medieval armour; but others are more original, with contemporary costumes and even the Menai Bridge and a railway locomotive on the brass to Robert Stephenson, also in Westminster Abbey. None of them, however, possess the vitality of the medieval and Renaissance brasses, nor do many of the restorations of old brasses, though some, such as a number of J. A. Waller's repairs at Cobham, Kent, are quite authentic in appearance.

At the beginning of this century a few William Morris style brasses were made (Morris was himself a keen brass-rubber), such as an attractive example in the Catholic church at Petworth, Sussex, dated 1901. However, the revival of brasses really came to an end soon after 1900 and later brasses, such as those made during the First World War, are not artistically important. Brass-making has dwindled to a few inscriptions by the time of writing. Brasses have not yet been adopted by twentieth-century art, but as they came late in the Gothic and Renaissance periods, so, too, they may yet be revived in a modern idiom.

# 5 ❊ The Brasses Themselves

K NIGHTS IN ARMOUR almost immediately spring to mind whenever
brasses are mentioned, and they are a very important category,
including the oldest and several of the finest of the brasses remaining
in England. Not all armoured figures, of course, were actually dubbed
knights, for the majority were only country squires, who had probably
never taken part in any fighting and may not even have possessed a complete
suit of armour. The Crusades were virtually over by the time that brasses
came into fashion (there is only one known brass to a Crusader—Sir Roger
de Trumpington, 1289) and from then until the Civil War there was not
much fighting to be done. The Hundred Years' War occupied only a small
proportion of English troops and the Wars of the Roses involved only the
barons' retainers; so for much of the time the only opportunity for military
service was with the knightly orders, such as the Teutonic Knights in
Lithuania, or in border skirmishes with Wales or Scotland. Nevertheless the
spirit of the feudal system if not the practice demanded that every Lord
of the Manor be a military man, ready to lead his followers into battle,
and social convention demanded that a man be shown on his brass in
full armour.

Brasses illustrate admirably the long struggle of armour against ever
improving weapons. The earliest brasses show armour that had hardly
changed since the Norman Conquest, but the later show how longbows,
crossbows and firearms forced armourers to sacrifice lightness and flexibility
for strength and solidity, until they gave up the unequal contest in the late
sixteenth century.

In the late thirteenth and early fourteenth centuries brasses show the last
years of complete suits of chain-mail, with little or no rigid defence—as on
the brasses at Stoke D'Abernon, Surrey, 1277; Trumpington near
Cambridge, 1289; Chartham near Canterbury, 1306; Acton near Long
Melford, Suffolk, c 1310 (Fig 8); two half-effigies, both c 1300, from Croft

*Fig 27.* Sir Richard de Buslingthorpe, c 1300, Buslingthorpe,
Lincolnshire (indents of inscription omitted)

near Skegness and Buslingthorpe near Market Rasen, Lincolnshire (Fig 27);
and a few incised slabs, such as at Sollars Hope near Hereford, c 1225.
These suits consisted of a hawberk, or coat of chain-mail reaching to the
knees, with a hood and mittens attached in such a way that they could be
thrown back, as is shown on the Chartham brass. The legs were clothed in
stockings of chain-mail over which were fixed knee-caps of steel or boiled
leather. The chain-mail was invariably made of rings of steel, riveted or
welded together. This made a very complicated pattern, which could be
represented on brasses by a number of conventions: on the Acton brass
each ring is shown linked to its fellows, at Buslingthorpe the rings are only
suggested by wavy lines, and on the Trumpington brass and nearly all
later examples, they are shown by rows of crescents set in alternate directions. This last convention is a fairly accurate representation of chain-mail
when it is stretched a little, and has nothing to do with 'laced' or 'banded'
mail, which was invented in the nineteenth century. The only other type of
mail is made up of little scales of steel laced together, which only appears
on a few details, such as the mittens of the Buslingthorpe knight.

To prevent mail chafing the skin or sharp links inflicting a wound when pushed into the skin by the point of a lance or arrow, a thick padded coat or *gambeson* was worn under the hawberk, and a padded coif under the hood, which gave the wearer a rather bulbous appearance. To keep the sun off the metal and prevent the heat of the armour from becoming intolerable, a cloth coat was worn over the hawberk; it was usually called a surcoat, or, when decorated with heraldic devices, a coat-of-arms. This was gathered at the waist by a tight cord, below which was worn a wide sword-belt, with an arrangement of straps to hold the sword conveniently. The sword was very large and heavy, used more as a hammer than a cutting blade, and was covered by a decorative scabbard. The other offensive weapon, the lance, was too long to appear on brasses, but a shortened lance is held by Sir John Daubernoun. Spurs at this time were simple spikes strapped on to the heels. The helmet is used as a pillow at Trumpington, and is worn only on the Sollars Hope incised slab.

Additional defences were *ailettes*, or little plates of steel or boiled leather which were fixed diagonally on the shoulders to protect the collar-bone from a downward blow. On brasses, however, they are shown flat behind the shoulders, since they would hardly be recognisable in perspective. At Trumpington and Chartham they are decorated with armorial bearings. The other rigid defence, the shield, was by this time reduced to a small almost triangular curved device, strapped on to the left arm and secured by a belt over the right shoulder. It is worn facing the front on the Stoke D'Abernon brass but moved round to the side on the others.

The next brasses, later in the fourteenth century, show a considerable amount of defensive plate for the limbs, but still a preponderance of mail. Those at Pebmarsh near Halstead, Essex, 1323 (Fig 28), and Gorleston near Great Yarmouth, c 1320 (Fig 29), are transitional. The Gorleston brass is remarkable in showing the mouth slightly open and the teeth exposed. A few years brings a new style of armour, represented at Westley Waterless near Newmarket, Cambridge, c 1325, and Stoke D'Abernon, Surrey, 1327 (Fig 30). Here there are tubular *vambraces* under the hawberk sleeves on the forearms and half-*rerebraces* over the mail on the upper arms, half greaves on the shins and jointed *sabatons* on the feet. Joints were protected by roundels of plate decorated with lions' faces. A small helmet, the *bascinet*, was worn on the top of the head, attached by laces to a wide collar of mail or *aventail*. The hawberk was covered by a coat made up of many small steel plates laced together and riveted to a cloth or leather cover, probably called a *brigandine*. The lower fringe of this appears beneath the surcoat, which is cut short in front and shows the successive layers of brigandine, hawberk and gambeson.

Fig 29. (?) Sir Adam de Bacon,
c 1320, Gorleston, Norfolk

*Fig 28.*   Sir William FitzRalph, 1323,
Pebmarsh, Essex

Spurs now developed into the more sophisticated rowell type, as is still used, with little spiked wheels. Shields by now had become hardly more than small decorative appendages, worn facing the front.

The brasses at Elsing near Dereham, Norfolk, 1347 (Fig 31), Wimbish near Saffron Walden, Essex, 1347 (page 49), and Bowers Gifford near Basildon, Essex, 1348, are transitional to the next major style. On these

*Fig 30.* Sir John Daubernoun,
1327, Stoke D'Abernon, Surrey

*Fig 31.* Sir Hugh Hastings, 1347,
Elsing, Norfolk

the back of the surcoat has also been cut short, leaving the form of garment
usually called a *jupon*. The three brasses have varying amounts of plate—
at Bowers Gifford there are vambraces, gauntlets, and thigh-defences or
*cuisses* made up of small plates fastened together in the same way as a
brigandine, and known as brigandine-work; but the shins are only covered
with chain-mail and the sleeves of the hawberk nearly cover the vambraces.

*Fig 32.* Sir John de Cobham,
c 1365, Cobham, Kent

*Fig 33.* Sir Morys and Isabel Russell,
1401, Dyrham, Gloucestershire

At Elsing there are cuisses of brigandine-work and half-tubes of plate over
the hawberk sleeves, while an old drawing shows that the shins were protected only by chain-mail. At Wimbish, however, the arms are completely
encased in steel and there are greaves strapped over the mail stockings. All
three have pointed bascinets, though the head at Bowers Gifford is lost. At
Elsing there is a visor and *beaver*, which, when closed, would cover the

face; but they are difficult to represent clearly and appear on very few brasses. Some variations in armour appear on the figures in the side-shafts of the Elsing brass, which also display a variety of weapons, swords, lances and a battle-axe.

Around 1360 a style of armour was developed which hardly changed externally until about 1410, as can be seen on the brasses at Cobham, Kent, c 1367, and Dyrham near Bristol, 1401 (Figs 32, 33). In the 1360s the jupon became a tight-fitting garment and revealed the scalloped edge of

*Fig 34.* Sir Thomas and Elizabeth
Camoys, 1419, Trotton, Sussex

the brigandine underneath, though soon after that it became longer and was itself scalloped. The fringe of the hawberk invariably shows below the jupon. About 1380 the brigandine gave way to a cuirass, consisting of solid breastplate and backplate, with a skirt of hoops on the hips. At Ingham, Norfolk, there was formerly a brass that omitted the jupon and showed the riveted cover of the brigandine, but this was stolen in the late nineteenth century. All surviving English brasses keep the jupon until the fifteenth century.

Cuisses of brigandine-work continued until about 1375, after which they gave way to plate encasing both arms and legs. Leather gauntlets studded with steel covered the hands. Roundels disappeared, leaving a patch of mail showing at the armpits. The sword belt was now usually straight across the middle and its right side held a dagger, called a *misericorde* because it was used to finish off wounded enemies. The sword hung straight at the left side and was rather smaller than before.

After about 1410 the jupon was dropped from nearly all brasses, though it is still shown at Amberley, Sussex, in 1424, where it has short sleeves. The bare plate armour was known as 'white armour', presumably because it shone in the sunlight. No chain-mail was now to be seen, since the aventail was replaced by a plate collar or *gorget*, and roundels reappeared at the armpits. The sword was now worn from a diagonal belt and the dagger was hooked on to the lowest hoop of the skirt. One of the finest examples of this fashion is the figure of Thomas, Baron Camoys, at Trotton, Sussex, 1419 (Fig 34). On this the edges of the plates are decorated with trefoils and rosettes appear on the roundels.

In the second half of the fifteenth century the increasing use of firearms made armour almost obsolete in war and so armourers concentrated more on jousting suits. The brasses at Ulcombe, Kent, 1470 (Fig 35), and St Albans Abbey, 1480, show this jousting-armour. The armour of the left shoulder was very strongly reinforced, since the point of the lance was to strike there, and the shoulder-plates sometimes overlapped in front and behind. Elbow-plates also became much larger and were curved and fluted to deflect the point of the lance. In contrast leg armour became more flexible, and the solid skirt of hoops gave place to a light skirt of chain-mail, overlapped by hanging plates or *tassets*. Helmets are now rarely shown on brasses, but where they do appear they are loose 'tin hats' or *sallets*. The Great Helm, worn only during the joust, is commonly used as a pillow. A few brasses show a further refinement of jousting-armour: a little hinged bracket on the right side of the breastplate, in which the lance was steadied during the charge.

After about 1480 real armour became much more complicated and

Fig 35.  Ralph and Anne St Leger, 1470, Ulcombe,
Kent

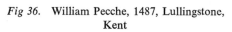

Fig 36.  William Pecche, 1487, Lullingstone,
Kent

elaborate and was richly decorated. Brass-engravers seem to have given up trying to represent the new styles and evolved a conventional armour that remained unchanged on brasses from about 1485 to 1545. A typical example can be seen at Lullingstone near Sevenoaks, Kent, 1487 (Fig 36). The armour is very simple and straightforward, with much the same elements as that just described, but rounded off. Shoes became broad-toed in armour as in civilian costume, a fashion said to have been started by the Emperor Maximilian to hide the fact that he had six toes. A great many brasses show the armour again covered with a form of surcoat, now always called a tabard, though in the Middle Ages this word applied to civilian and academic gowns as well as military. It is probably better to call it a *heraldic* tabard, since it is always emblazoned with a coat-of-arms on military figures.

In the mid-sixteenth century armour is again shown realistically on brasses and ceremonial armour is well represented. Since jousting was now prohibited and armour was almost useless for war, Elizabethan and later armour was made only as a ceremonial uniform and consequently became lighter, more flexible and ornamental. A good example is the brass to John Gage at Firle near Lewes, 1595 (Fig 3), showing the long articulated tassets, jointed breastplate, padded breeches and elegant swinging rapier. The edges of the plates are frilled and the neck and wrists finished off with the inevitable ruff.

During the first half of the seventeenth century the tassets grew even longer and leg armour was often omitted, being replaced by knee breeches and jackboots, as on the brass to Sir Edward Filmer at East Sutton near Maidstone, Kent, 1629. The ruff disappears around 1630, when the brass to Richard Barttelot of Stopham near Pulborough, Sussex was engraved (Fig 37), and is replaced by a turned-down collar.

During the Civil War most of the soldiers wore little or no metal armour, but a leather coat, as appears on the figure of George Hodges, c 1630, at Wedmore, Somerset (Fig 38), was some protection. He has a narrow metal gorget but no other armour, and carries a pike.

A few officers wore half-armour, with no leg-pieces, as does Ralph Assheton, 1650, at Middleton, Lancashire. He was general of the Parliamentary forces in the county of Lancashire, and left a rare example of a Cromwellian brass. The few later military brasses show half-armour, except for Nicholas Toke of Great Chart near Ashford, Kent, 1680 (Fig 21), who is dressed in the full armour of his youth.

Victorian military brasses are mostly rather disappointing, since the gorgeous regimental uniforms are not shown and soldiers are dressed very simply or in the armour of the Middle Ages. A few twentieth-century brasses to soldiers of the First World War, such as those at Cheriton near Folkestone, Kent, or Sledmere, Yorkshire, show figures in khaki uniforms.

Medieval armour was frequently used for heraldic display. Armorial devices appear on the surcoat and its various forms, the shield, ailettes, scabbard, sword hilt and lance pennon. Occasionaly heraldic animals are placed at the feet of figures, though the choice is usually restricted to the lion, symbol of knightly courage and the hound, symbol of manly sport.

Military decorations were few in the Middle Ages and consisted chiefly of two collars awarded by the houses of York and Lancaster. Lancaster's collar was the *collar of SS*, a chain of S-shaped links of uncertain

*Fig 37.* Richard, Mary and Rose
Barttelot, c 1630, Stopham, Sussex

*Fig 38.* George Hodges, c 1630,
Wedmore, Somerset

significance (Fig 73m), which continued in use after the fall of the house of Lancaster and is still worn by some officials. York's collar was made up of suns and roses, as on the brass of Sir Anthony Grey at St Albans Abbey, 1480. Other collars, such as the collar of mermaids at Wotton-under-Edge, Gloucestershire, were private heraldic devices. The only other major military decoration was the famous Garter, which is worn below the left knee at Trotton, Sussex (Fig 34) and on a few other brasses. The full Garter robes are shown only on the brass of Sir Thomas Bullen at Hever, Kent (frontispiece), and consist of a blue mantle with the badge of the Garter on the shoulder, a red sash and a solid gold collar of gartered roses. A few other brasses show only the mantle, as at Little Easton, Essex, and this is also worn by canons of Windsor who were all members of the Order. The brass of Ralph, Lord Cromwell at Tattershall, Lincolnshire, once so dressed, has been strangely mutilated: the badge of the Garter on the shoulder and the Garter itself round the leg have been cut out of the brass. Military trophies, in the form of captured ensigns, are shown on a few brasses, as at Wedmore, Somerset, c 1630 (Fig 39); and Sir Simon Felbrigg of Felbrigg near Cromer, Norfolk, is shown holding the Royal Standard, since he was standard-bearer to Richard II.

## ECCLESIASTICAL BRASSES

A great many pre-Reformation brasses show ecclesiastics in their liturgical vestments, whose pattern hardly changed from the thirteenth to the sixteenth centuries. The only development is one of style, since by the sixteenth century drapery had become stiff instead of falling naturally as it does on earlier brasses, and the decline in draughtsmanship is evident as in all other brasses.

There are seven orders of clergy, all distinguished by the tonsure, a bald patch shaved off the top of the head, often covered by a skullcap. Of the four minor orders—doorkeeper, reader, exorcist and acolyte—there are no identifiable brasses, though a few figures in civil dress with tonsures may be in minor orders. Angels, however, when they appear with incense or on either side of a head, are mostly dressed as acolytes in an *amice*, or linen hood, usually edged with a stiff strip of embroidery or *apparel*, appearing as a collar round the neck, and an *alb*, a straight white robe fastened with a cord or *cingulum*.

The major orders—subdeacon, deacon and priest—wear amice and alb, the latter usually adorned with patches of embroidery (also known as apparels) on the cuffs, the back and front of the lower hems, and the breast. Over this the subdeacon wears a *tunicle*, a long-sleeved gown with slits at the sides, and a *maniple*, a strip of cloth hanging over the left arm; whereas the deacon wears a *stole*, a long strip of cloth worn as a sash across the left shoulder, as well as a maniple, both practically obscured by a *dalmatic*, which is almost identical with the tunicle except that it is usually more adorned, having H-shaped strips of embroidery or *orphreys* on back and front. There are no brasses surviving to deacons or subdeacons, but whenever a deacon-saint such as St Stephen or St Lawrence appears on a brass, he is dressed appropriately, as on the brass at Castle Ashby, near Northampton, 1401.

Most ecclesiastical brasses are to priests, who wear amice, alb, cingulum, stole (worn straight round the neck, crossed over the breast and held in place by the cingulum), maniple, and over all the *chasuble*, originally a bell-shaped garment with a hole for the head, but usually by the late Middle

*Fig 39.* Thomas Hodges, c 1630, Wedmore, Somerset

*Fig 40.* Nicholas Kaerwent, 1381, Crondall, Hampshire

Ages cut away at the sides to have less weight on the arms. The earliest brasses show a plain chasuble, but later chasubles are decorated with orphreys round the hem and forming a Y-shape on back and front. The chasuble, stole, maniple and sometimes the apparels of the amice and alb, form matching sets that vary in colour with the liturgical season, though the colour is never shown on brasses. On some elaborate brasses the orphreys of the chasuble are very wide and ornate, sometimes with a row of saints down the middle. A good typical brass to a priest is at Crondall, Hampshire, 1381 (Fig 40).

There are few brasses to bishops, since they were mostly destroyed when the great cathedrals were plundered. The few that remain are resplendent in all the eucharistic vestments of the priest, together with the tunicle and dalmatic worn under the chasuble and the distinctive garments of the office of bishop—embroidered sandals, gloves cut to show the ring underneath, and the mitre with two ribbons or *infulae* hanging down at the back. The mitre is the only exception to the conservatism of ecclesiastical dress, for the earliest brasses show it low-peaked, and it gradually rose, becoming more elaborate and higher, until it became bulbous. The crozier or pastoral staff, with a crook-shaped head and sometimes a veil or *vexillum* hanging from it, is carried in the left hand, while the right hand is usually shown blessing. One of the earliest surviving examples is in Hereford Cathedral to Bishop Trellick, 1360 (Fig 41).

*Fig 41.* Bishop John Trellick, 1360, Hereford Cathedral (canopy and inscription, restored, omitted)

*Fig 42.* Archbishop Robert Waldeby, 1397, Westminster Abbey (canopy and inscription omitted)

*Fig 43.* Chalice, c 1520, Old
Buckenham, Norfolk

*Fig 44.* Walter Hewke, c 1510, Trinity Hall,
Cambridge

Archbishops, to whom only three brasses survive in England, are distinguished by the *pallium,* or circle of white lamb's wool worn round the neck
with long pendants at back and front, and a cross instead of a crozier, as
on the brass to Archbishop Waldeby of York from Westminster Abbey,
1397 (Fig 42). No brasses to cardinals survive in England, though there is
an indent in Canterbury Cathedral showing a cardinal's hat.

Many priests are shown holding the chalice and Host, which appear
without any effigy on several East Anglian brasses, as at Old Buckenham,
near Attleborough, Norfolk, c 1520 (Fig 43).

In addition to the eucharistic vestments, priests are frequently shown in processional vestments, worn over a cassock. These are the *surplice*, which is really a smaller alb; an *almuce* or fur hood with long pendants in front; and a large cloak or cope fastened by a clasp or *morse*, and with a vestigial hood at the back. The fur of the almuce is usually represented on a brass by lead inlays. This vestment, now obsolete, was normally worn only by canons, but its use was extended to parish priests in England alone. The cope was the richest and most elaborate garment, with wide embroidered orphreys down the front, sometimes with rows of saints, as at Trinity Hall, Cambridge, c 1510 (Fig 44). Some copes are made of patterned brocades, as at The Queen's College, Oxford, 1518, and others are marked with personal initials or emblems, such as the maple leaves on the cope of John Mapilton at Broadwater near Worthing, Sussex, 1432. A few brasses to priests show surplice and almuce without the cope, as does that to Canon Coorthorpe in Oxford Cathedral, 1557.

Two or three brasses show priests vested for a funeral, wearing the amice, alb, stole and maniple, which they would wear at the Requiem Mass, but with a cope instead of a chasuble, as the actual burial is not a liturgical function. Technically the maniple should not be worn, and its appearance on these brasses may be a designer's error or an obsolete usage. An example is at Horsham, Sussex, 1427 (Fig 45). A few priests are shown simply in their everyday dress, a cassock or soutane, and several others are shown in university gowns.

A few brasses to the religious orders still exist, though most of them were destroyed. At the time of the Dissolution monks vested for Mass in the same way as secular priests and Benedictine abbots are dressed exactly as bishops; but there are some brasses left showing religious habits. Most of these are to Benedictines or Cluniacs, who dressed in the same way, all in black. The tunic and scapula are hidden on brasses by the cowl, the voluminous gown with broad sleeves worn for liturgical occasions, over which appears the wide hood with folds hanging down in front. A typical example is in St Albans Abbey to Dom Robert Beaunor, c 1460 (Fig 46), a Benedictine; while the huge brass at Cowfold to Prior Nelond of Lewes, Sussex, 1433, shows the identical Cluniac habit. Of the other orders of monks, no brasses survive to Cistercians, though there are indents in the ruins of Cistercian abbeys such as Fountains; and there never were any brasses to Carthusians since they are forbidden to have personal monuments. Friars, by their vow of complete poverty, could not normally have brasses, and the few that exist must have been made by the friary to commemorate particularly holy brothers. Since the brass to the Franciscan friar at Great Amwell, Hertfordshire, was stolen in 1968, the only survivor

*Fig 45.* Thomas Clarke, 1427, Horsham, Sussex (largely restored)

*Fig 46.* Robert Beaunor, c 1460, St Alban's Abbey

is a half-effigy engraved on a lectern at Yeovil, Somerset, c 1460 (Fig 47). But there are two palimpsests with friars on the reverse—one at Halvergate near Norwich with a half-effigy, and the other at Denham, Buckinghamshire, with a mutilated full length figure (Fig 48); both are set in hinged frames so that the reverses are visible, and show the Franciscan habit of a plain tunic held by a knotted cord, and a hood, very like civilian costume of the time. The Great Amwell figure showed the sandals and the Denham friar illustrates the posture of prayer common in the religious orders, with the hands folded inside the tunic sleeves.

The canons regular are represented by an Augustinian canon at Upper Winchendon near Aylesbury, Buckinghamshire, 1502, and two abbots—at South Creake, Norfolk, 1509, and Dorchester Abbey, Oxfordshire, c 1510. All wear cassock, surplice, almuce and plain cloak or 'choir-cope', and the abbots hold croziers.

Nuns are even rarer than monks on brasses and when they do appear they wear plain gowns, veils and wimples, very like the earliest civilian ladies. There are two abbesses with croziers, and a prioress at Nether Wallop, Hampshire, 1436 (Fig 49). Widows, especially those who had vowed not to marry again, known as 'vowesses', are dressed in the same way.

After the Reformation, Mass vestments were banned, though there are isolated examples as late as 1579, when a bishop at Tideswell, Derbyshire, is shown in full pontificals; but processional vestments, usually without the

*Fig 47.*   Martin Forester, c 1460, Yeovil, Somerset

Fig 49. Mary Gore, 1436, Nether Wallop, Hampshire

*Fig 48.* John Pyke, c 1440, on back of palimpsest at Denham, Buckinghamshire

cope, survive for some time, as on the brass of Canon Coorthorpe already mentioned. Bishop Geste of Salisbury Cathedral, 1578, and Bishop Robinson of Carlisle at The Queen's College, Oxford, 1616 (Fig 26), are dressed in a *rochet* or long surplice, and *chimere* or sleeveless coat open at the front. Bishop Robinson holds a crozier but Bishop Geste has only a short staff. On the other hand Archbishop Harsnett of York at Chigwell, Essex, 1631 (Fig 1), wears a rich cope and mitre as well as rochet and chimere. There are a few brasses showing mitres without figures, such as one in Wells Cathedral to Bishop Lake, 1626.

After Queen Elizabeth's reign, ecclesiastics are usually shown in lay dress, though some wear cassock and scarf, and others wear university gowns with square caps, as does Dean Wythines of Battle, Sussex, 1615 (Fig 50). Many clergy are shown with their wives, and even as early as Queen Elizabeth's reign, there are at least two brasses to bishops' wives.

Modern ecclesiastics on brasses are usually shown in vestments, though Dean Burgon of Chichester, 1888, is dressed in cassock, surplice and scarf. In the crypt of Ampleforth Abbey church, Yorkshire, is a large and fine brass to a bishop, dated 1915, showing full pontificals and several other modern ecclesiastical brasses can be found in the great Abbey churches.

CIVILIAN BRASSES

The earliest are to ladies: a large elaborate brass that formerly had a canopy at Trotton near Midhurst, Sussex (Fig 9), and a small figure at Pitstone, Buckinghamshire, near Tring, both c 1310. A third contemporary figure was stolen from Sedgefield, Durham, in 1969. They are dressed simply in a kirtle or close-fitting gown with buttoned sleeves, a surcoat or similar gown worn over the kirtle with shorter sleeves, a veil, and a wimple (a linen covering round the head, neck and throat). This costume remained virtually unchanged on brasses until c 1370, except that a few ladies, such as Lady de Creke at Westley Waterless near Newmarket, wear a cloak or mantle.

Male civilians are first represented c 1325 at East Wickham near Greenwich, London, and are also simply dressed, usually in a straight gown then also called a kirtle, sometimes with strips of cloth hanging from the elbows, a hood attached to a small cape and pointed shoes, as at Taplow, Buckinghamshire, c 1350 (Fig 10). Manuscript illustrations show that these clothes were brightly coloured, though the brasses do not represent this. By 1360 the gown was buttoned down the front and sleeves, sometimes with an incredible number of tiny buttons.

After about 1370, women are usually shown without the wimple, with the hair done up in one net on the head and small nets on the shoulders. The surcoat in many cases was cut away at the sides to show the kirtle, and at Lingfield, Surrey, 1375, the kirtle is shown in a different colour to distinguish the two garments. A few women, as at Bray near Maidenhead, Berkshire, had strips of cloth hanging from their elbows in imitation of male costume; others dispensed with the surcoat altogether and are shown in kirtle and mantle.

By 1400 men usually wore an overgown or tabard, buttoned down the front, with the cuffs of the kirtle protruding from it and covering half the

HIC IACET IOHANNES WYTHINES IN TPÆ
NOBILI CIVITATE CESTRIÆ NATVS ET IN
ACADEMIA OXON EDVCATVS IBIQVE ÆNI
NASI COLLEGIJ SOCIVS SACRÆ THEOLOGIÆ
DOCTOR ACADEMIEQ OXON PRÆDICÆ I
VICECANCELLARIVS HVIVSQ EC CLESIÆ DE
BATTEL XLIJ ANNOS DECANVS QVI OBIJT
XVIIJ DIE MARTIJ ANNO ÆTATIS SVÆ 84
ET SALVTIS HVMANÆ 1615

QVÆDVM VOLVNT NOLVNTQ SI CHRISTE VOLEBAS
NEC MIHI VITA BREVIS NEC MIHI LONGA FVIT
VIVO TIBI MORIORQ TIBI TIBI CHRISTE RESVRGAM
MORI VVS ET VIVVS SVM MANEOQ TVVS

*Fig 50.* John Wythines, 1615, Battle, Sussex

*Fig 51.* Civilian, 1394, Hereford Cathedral

hands. At Hereford Cathedral, 1394 (Fig 51), the tabard is buttoned tight at the wrists.

The sideless surcoat had gone out of fashion by 1400, though a few examples occur as late as 1480, and women are usually dressed in a kirtle, now completely covered by a high- or low-necked surcoat, with or without a mantle. Men's gowns were unchanged but the richer merchants wore a long cloak fastened on the right shoulder and an elaborate belt. Many grew forked beards, reminiscent of Chaucer's 'marchant with a forkéd berd'.

Civilian costume during the fifteenth century hardly changed except for ladies' headdresses. A few men wore short gowns showing hose underneath, as at Hildersham near Balsham, Cambridgeshire, 1408, and Taplow, Buckinghamshire, 1455 (Fig 52), but otherwise they are dressed in long gowns, sometimes edged with fur, with wide sleeves narrowing at the wrist to form pockets, said to have been known as 'devil's receptacles', because stolen objects could easily be hidden in them. Many wore purses at their belts, usually next to a dagger to protect them. Very few have beards.

Ladies wore a bewildering array of headdresses. Widows, such as Eleanor, Duchess of Gloucester, 1399, in Westminster Abbey (Fig 11); and servants, such as Katherine Stocket, maid to Eleanor, Lady Cobham, c 1420, at Lingfield, Surrey; still wore a plain veil and wimple. Unmarried girls had long flowing hair, as at Taplow (Fig 52), but married ladies had very elaborate headgear. In the first quarter of the fifteenth century the hair was usually done up in embroidered nets on either side of the head and covered with a crimped veil; this style appears on the brass to Lady Camoys at Trotton, Sussex, 1419 (Fig 34). The nets on each side grew gradually taller

*Fig 52*. Richard, Isabel and John Manfield, 1455, Taplow, Buckinghamshire

*Fig 53.*   John Croston and three wives, c 1470, Swinbrook, Oxfordshire

until, about the middle of the century, a horned effect was produced, as at
Swinbrook near Burford, Oxfordshire, c 1470 (Fig 53). Between 1470 and
1480 the horned headdress developed into its most fantastic and elegant
form, in which the hair was combed right back and a veil supported on
wire frames formed 'butterfly wings' behind the head, as at East Malling
near Maidstone, Kent, 1479 (Fig 54). To show off the shape of this headdress, the figures were turned sideways. Soon after 1480, however, this
lovely fashion gave place to a severe and uninteresting headdress which
framed the face with a kennel-like gable. The hood behind this was often
coloured on brasses where the figure is shown turned sideways.

The sixteenth century saw much greater change in civilian costume. Men's
gowns came to be open at the front and thickly lined and edged with fur,
often with false sleeves, while, beneath them, the undergown grew shorter
and shorter until by the middle of the century it was only a short jacket

G

*Fig 54.* Thomas and Iseult
Selby, 1479, East Malling,
Kent

over padded breeches and hose and broad-toed shoes. Many men wore pointed or broad beards and moustaches, which remained in fashion up to the Civil War. Unfortunately the quality of brass-design was not high enough at this time to show the elaborate court costumes of the beginning of Queen Elizabeth's reign.

In the early part of the sixteenth century many ladies emulated the heraldic display of their husbands' military tabards and wore their own and their husbands' arms on their clothes. A few brasses show heraldic ladies' costumes as early as the fourteenth century but they did not become popular until Henry VIII's reign and died out soon afterwards. Legh's *Armory* of 1597 states that 'Gentlewomen under the degree of a countesse have armes on Taberts, but the countesse and so upwards shal have their Armes in surcotes and mantels'. This distinction, however, was not observed, for nearly all ladies of all ranks, wore arms on their mantles and sometimes on their surcoats as well, and only one 'gentlewoman' wears a tabard—at Burton near Petworth, Sussex, 1558 (Fig 56). A typical example of a heraldic mantle can be seen at St Helen's, Bishopsgate, London, c 1535 (Fig 55).

After about 1530, ladies' surcoats changed in cut and the sleeves grew wide to show the slashed undersleeves of the kirtle. The headdress became shorter and less kennel-like. This is well represented on the figure of Agnes Andrews, 1541, at Charwelton near Daventry, Northamptonshire (Fig 57). (The figure of her husband is an 'appropriation' from c 1510.)

*Fig 56.* Elizabeth Goring, 1558, Burton, Sussex (other parts and indents omitted)

*Fig 55.* Lady, c 1535, St Helen's Bishopsgate, London

Succeeding the gabled headdress about 1550 came the 'Paris cap' or 'Mary Queen of Scots cap'—tight-fitting with a veil hanging behind. This was worn with a ruff and survived, with variations, until the seventeenth century. The kirtle and surcoat finally disappeared to be replaced by a farthingale—a hooped skirt, usually richly embroidered but mostly covered by a coat which was either loose and straight as on the Gage brasses (Fig 3) or bound in at the waist under a pointed stomacher, as on the elaborate

Fig 57. Thomas and Agnes Andrews, 1541, Charwelton, Northamptonshire

costume of Radcliff Wingfield, 1601, at Easton near Wickham Market, Suffolk (Fig 58).

Male costume of the late sixteenth century is well illustrated by the brass to Edward Gage and his family at Framfield near Uckfield, Sussex, 1595 (Fig 59): Edward Gage wears a doublet buttoned to the throat and a long gown closed at the front, with false sleeves and a ruff, while his son is gallantly dressed in a wide ruff, spotted doublet, padded breeches, hose and short cloak. The gown with false sleeves remained a feature of dignified civilian dress until the Civil War, though the ruff gradually gave place to a more sober collar. Less Puritanical people, and children shown as subsidiary figures, are dressed in doublet, knee-breeches, jackboots and a short cloak, as on the brass to William Randolph, 1641, at Biddenden, Kent.

Ladies' costume remained much the same until the Civil War, except that the farthingale tended to disappear in favour of a straight-falling dress. The wives of Richard Barttelot (Fig 37) from Stopham near Pulborough, Sussex, engraved c 1630, are dressed in long gowns, ruffs and veiled caps. Mrs Kenwellmersh, 1633, shown with her grandson Meneleb at Henfield,

*Fig 59.* Edward and Margaret Gage, 1595, Framfield, Sussex

*Fig 60.* Ann Kenwellmersh and Meneleb Rainsford, 1633, Henfield, Sussex

*Fig 58.* Radcliff Wingfield, 1601, Easton, Suffolk

HERE LYETH THE BODY OF Mrs ANN KENWELL-
MERSH A VERTVOVS & WOORTHY MATRON OF
PIETIE WHO DYED IN THE 68th YEER OF HER AGE
ANNO DNI: 1633
HERE ALSOE LYETH THE BODY OF MENELEB
RAINSFORD HER GRANDCHILD, THE SONNE OF HER
DAVGHTER MARY WHO DEPARTED HENCE ON THE
21th DAY OF MAY ANNO DNI: 1627, IN THE 9th
YEER OF HIS AGE

HERE LYETH BVRIED RADCLIFF WINGFELD THE WIFE
OF THOMAS WINGFELD OF EASTON ESQVIER A DAVGHTER
OF Sr GILBERT GERRARDE KNIGHT OF BROMLEY GRE
HARDE IN STAFFORDE SHIRE SOME TYME MASTER OF THE
ROWLES, & OF DAME ANNE GERRARDE HIS WYFE, WHICH
SAIDE RADCLIFF DYED THE XVIII DAYE OF IVLY 1601.

GREAT IOVE, HATH LOST HIS GANYMEDE I KNOW
WHICH MADE HIM SEEK AN OTHER HERE BELOW
AND FINDINGE NONE, NOT ONE LIKE VNTO THIS
HATH TANE HIM HENCE INTO ETERNALL BLISS
CEASE THEN FOR THY DEER MENELEB TO WEEP
GODS DARLINGE WAS, TOO GOOD FOR THEE TO KEEP
BVT RATHER IOYE IN THIS GREAT FAVOVR GIVEN
A CHILD ON EARTH IS MADE A SAINT IN HEAVEN

Sussex, wears a very wide ruff and carries a feather fan (Fig 60). Many ladies of this period wear 'steeple-crowned' hats.

After the Civil War there are very few civilian brasses. Mrs Williams of Pimperne near Blandford Forum, Dorset, 1694, wears a flowing dress, a pointed stomacher and loose veil. The last two brasses of the eighteenth century, at St Mary Cray near Orpington, South London, show Philadelphia Greenwood, 1747, in a shapeless dress and veil and Benjamin Greenwood, 1773, in a jacket, waistcoat, breeches, stockings and wig. Victorians, such as Robert Stephenson in Westminster Abbey, are shown rather non-committally in straight gowns.

## MISCELLANEOUS FIGURES

Legal costume is chiefly represented on brasses by judges and sergeants-at-law. Judges are almost invariably shown in a long straight gown, like the civilian gowns of the period but usually without belts, and a large cloak or mantle lined with minever, which is represented on brasses by lead inlays. The use of minever—a fur made from Siberian squirrels—was restricted by law to justices. A hood with a short cape and a close-fitting white cloth cap, known as a coif, completed the costume. The coif was the only distinctive garment, though the minever lining differentiated the wearer from ordinary people. A fine example of a judge's robes is shown on the brass to Sir John Cassy, 1400, at Deerhurst near Tewkesbury, Gloucestershire (Fig 61).

The sergeants-at-law also wore coifs, but instead of mantles they wore sleeved tabards over their gowns and hoods with rather wider capes than those of the judges. The coif alone distinguishes them from academics. An example of their costume is found on the brass to John Brook, sergeant-at-law, at St Mary Redcliffe, Bristol, 1522. He was also, according to the inscription, chief steward of Glastonbury Abbey, illustrating the close connection between the church and the law.

Other legal brasses, such as that of a barrister in the Temple Church, London, show ordinary civil costume. Notaries (solicitors), such as two at St Mary Tower, Ipswich, are dressed in civilian gowns with a pen-case and inkhorn hanging from the belt.

Academic gowns are, as might be expected, most frequently shown on brasses in and around Oxford and Cambridge, though there are isolated examples all over the country. Unfortunately the main distinction in dress between classes of graduate was one of colour, and since nearly all colour has been lost from brasses, it is difficult to differentiate between them. Certain general characteristics, however, can be recognised.

Nearly all academic brasses pre-date the Reformation when most

Fig 61. John and Alice Cassy, 1400,
Deerhurst, Gloucestershire

Fig 62. Doctor of Divinity, c 1500,
St Helen's Bishopsgate, London

graduates were priests, and so a common feature is the tonsure, and a cassock is the basic garment. Over this was worn a gown and a hood and sometimes an academic cap. Parts of these may be cut away to take inlays of colour or lead. The most distinctive type of gown is the *cappa clausa*, worn by doctors of decretals (Papal decrees) and by professors of sacred theology, which was a bell-shaped garment without sleeves, reaching to the ground, with a single slit in front for the arms. The hood to go with it is represented on brasses by lead fillings, indicating fur all over. A typical example is the anonymous figure at St Helen's Bishopsgate, London (Fig 62).

*Fig 63.* John Bloxham
and John Whytton,
c 1420, Merton College,
Oxford

*Fig 64.* John Motesfont, 1420, Lydd, Kent

Another type of cappa, with two arm-slits, is shown on a few brasses, such
as that to John Lowthe, Professor of Civil Law, 1427, at New College,
Oxford, where the ends of two long sleeves appear as if from behind, and
to John Bloxham, MA, at Merton College (Fig 63). Most masters of arts,

however, wear a sleeveless gown, with the wide sleeves of the cassock coming through slits at the sides. A large number of bachelors and 'Scholars of Sacred Theology' wear a sort of tabard with wide sleeves ending at the elbow, and a hood lined with fur, as at Lydd, Kent, 1420 (Fig 64). A few brasses show gowns with long sleeves to the wrists like a cassock but apparently without any distinction between classes of graduate. In all cases there are exceptions but as so many brasses of academics, particularly in Oxford, have been separated from their inscriptions or relaid, it is difficult to know whether the attributions are now muddled or whether, as it certainly appears, the medieval engravers were inconsistent.

The forms of the hood and cap are at least constant. The hood has a wide cape and hangs down with a long point, which is shown clearly on kneeling figures such as John Strete, 1405, from Upper Hardres near Canterbury. The cap is shaped like a tight-fitting beret with a point on top and is often shown with fillings representing fur or colouring.

There is only one known brass to a medieval undergraduate, strangely located in All Souls' College, Oxford, and showing him in an ordinary cloak and hood. Schoolboys are shown on a few brasses, as at Headbourne Worthy to a scholar of nearby Winchester, who is wearing ordinary civilian clothes.

After the Reformation the forms of the gowns changed slightly, many of them becoming open-fronted. They are hardly distinguishable from the gowns of the ordinary populace. The hood by 1600 had evolved into its modern form and the cap, though not often shown, is square, almost a mortar-board, as on the brass to Dean Wythines of Battle, already mentioned (Fig 50). John Pendarves, a commoner of Exeter College, in St Michael's church, Oxford, 1617, is shown on his brass in a sleeveless buttoned gown and an enormous ruff and is disputing, book in hand (Fig 15).

Livery collars and badges are shown on a few brasses to retainers of the Crown or some noble family. The ordinary form of livery collar was a loose strip of cloth round the neck, fastened in front. It was always coloured, probably following the heraldic colours of the lord who gave it. A typical example is shown on the brass to Richard Manfield of Taplow, Buckinghamshire (Fig 52). The collar is worn also by marshals of the hall to the Earl of Arundel, such as Richard Barttelot of Stopham near Pulborough, 1482 (Fig 65), who holds between his hands the white marshal's baton. Royal liveries, with the badge of rose and crown, are shown on brasses to yeomen of the guard, as at East Wickham near Greenwich, 1568; sergeants-at-arms, as at Wandsworth, London, 1420; and yeomen of the crown, as on a brass in the possession of the Society of Antiquaries in London. Civic mantles,

Fig 66.    James    Grey,    1591,    Hunsdon,
Hertfordshire

Fig 65.    Richard and Petronella Barttelot,
1482, Stopham, Sussex

lined with red, are worn by mayors and aldermen on a few brasses, such
as those at St Peter's, Colchester, where the colouring survives. A late
nineteenth-century brass in St Paul's Cathedral shows a lord mayor in a
cocked hat with his chain of office.

A number of other professions are distinguishable on brasses only by
their attributes or instruments, which are usually placed under the feet of
the figure: for example, wool merchants from East Anglia or the West of
England usually have their feet on a woolsack or sheep, as at Northleach,
Gloucestershire; a vintner on an incised slab in Hereford Cathedral has a
cask; while a tailor of Gloucester, also at Northleach, has scissors on the
grassy mound beneath his feet. The fishmonger from Taplow, Buckinghamshire has a fish at the foot of his cross (Fig 10). Several gamekeepers are
shown in hunting dress, with horn and bow, as at Hunsdon near Ware,
Hertfordshire, where the keeper is shown shooting a deer, while Death

stabs them both (Fig 66). At Rotherhithe, London, and Beeston Regis near Cromer, Norfolk, can be found brasses to seamen: the second has a boatswain's pipe hanging from his belt.

Infant mortality was high in the Middle Ages and there are many brasses showing infants in swaddling clothes, known as 'chrysom children', who died within a month of their baptism. They appear either on their own or, more usually, beside or in the arms of their parents, as at Cranbrook, Kent, 1520 (Fig 67). A few seventeenth-century brasses show mothers who died in childbirth in four-poster beds with the children in swaddling clothes beside them, as at Wormington, Gloucestershire, near Evesham (Fig 16). At St Cross, Holywell, Oxford, a mother 'who dangerously escaping death at 3 severall travells in childe-bed died together w$^{th}$ the fourth', is shown in bed with three children in shrouds and the fourth in swaddling clothes. Another interesting brass to an infant, Arthur Wharton, 1642, at Wooburn, Buckinghamshire, shows him in a long gown holding a rose and lying on a tomb with this verse inscribed on it:

> Nine months wrought me in y$^e$ wombe,
> Nine more brought me to this tombe.

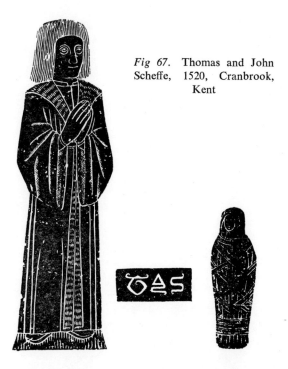

*Fig 67.* Thomas and John Scheffe, 1520, Cranbrook, Kent

Fig 69.   Mary   Howard,   1638,
Firle, Sussex

Fig 68.   Thomasine
Tendring, 1485, Yoxford,
Suffolk

HERE LYETH. THE BODY OF MARY HOWARD
DAVGHTER OF WILLIAM LORD EVRE SHE DIED
AT FIRLE THE 28 OF IANVARIE ANNO DNI 1638
AGED 36. YEARES WHEN SHE HAD BENNE MARIED
18 YEARES WANTING A QVARTER TO SR WILLIAM
HOWARD ELDEST SONNE TO S PHILIPP HOWARD
SONNE & HEIRE TO Y LORD WILLIAM HOWARD
YONGEST SONNE TO Y DVKE OF NORFOLKE

Let an infant teach thee (Man)
Since this life is but a Span
Use it so thou maiest be
Happy in yᵉ next with me.

   A peculiar type of brass, to which reference has already been made, is
the shrouded figure or skeleton, which was common during the fifteenth
and sixteenth centuries, and was designed as a 'memento mori'. It was

derived from stone tombs that showed an effigy in normal dress on top, and, glimpsed through arcading on the side, a shrouded and emaciated corpse below. Brasses, however, do not usually show both normal and shrouded figures in this way, but a shrouded figure only. The shroud was a single sheet, knotted at the head and feet, and usually drawn together at the front. Sometimes it was marked with a cross over the head, as at Taplow, Buckinghamshire, where John Manfield is shown in a shroud beside his brother and sister in ordinary dress (Fig 52). Shrouded figures cover all classes, including priests, as at Bodiam, Sussex; one of the finest is at Yoxford, Suffolk, where Thomasine Tendring is shown in a shroud with her children beside her, some in shrouds and some, who survived her, in normal dress (Fig 68). Although shroud brasses could be dignified they were often merely gruesome, without any artistic or moral worth. They coincided with the worst period of brass-engraving, and so there are few attractive examples. An exception is that already described to Mary Howard, 1638, at Firle near Lewes, Sussex (Fig 69), where the shroud nearly envelops the body and the figure appears calm and dignified.

As well as shrouded corpses there are several skeletons on brasses, some with shrouds, some without, and all rather inaccurately drawn. They continued long after shroud brasses had died out and were very popular in the seventeenth and eighteenth centuries. The brass to Dorothy Williams, 1694, from Pimperne, Dorset, shows a skeleton with a clothed figure, presumably representing the soul, rising from it (Fig 22); and two little eighteenth-century brasses at Bibury, Gloucestershire, show recumbent skeletons (Fig 70). Skulls or crossed bones are much more common and

*Fig 70.*   John Matthews, 1707, Bibury, Gloucestershire

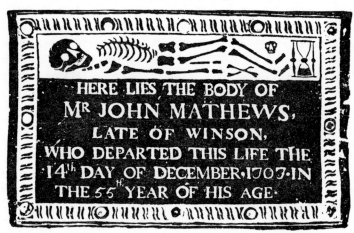

appear, together with scythes, hourglasses, sexton's spades and worms on several late brasses. Often the figure of Death as a skeleton appears, as on the brasses from Shepton Mallet and Hunsdon already described (Figs 17, 66). The final indignity, a shrouded and rotting corpse being eaten by worms, is shown only on one brass, at Oddington, near Oxford, c 1510.

### FOREIGN BRASSES IN ENGLAND

Nearly all these brasses are to be found within easy reach of the English coast facing Flanders. Scotland was also rich in Flemish brasses and incised slabs, though only one brass survives; they were imported during the Middle Ages when Scotland was not on good enough terms with England to import English brasses, and the record of some of these importations has already been described in Chapter 2.

Nearly all foreign brasses in Britain are Flemish in origin and closely parallel the many fine examples that survive in Flemish churches. Bruges was a major centre for brass-work and its brasses can be found as far apart as Portugal and Denmark. There are also a few brasses in the south of England that are probably French, though our knowledge of French styles of engraving is restricted to what can be deduced from indents and pre-Revolution drawings. The other main categories of Continental brasses, German and Silesian, are not represented in England since Flanders and France were nearer sources of supply.

The Continental brass was conceived on very different lines from the English. Socially it was confined to the ruling class. It was always large and expensive, and designed to be as impressive and overpowering as possible. The design was treated as a rectangle to be filled with decoration, and canopies with an abundance of pinnacles and niches placed against elaborately diapered backgrounds are prominent features. The largest Flemish brasses in England are at King's Lynn, Norfolk, 1349 and 1364; Newark, Nottinghamshire, 1361; St Albans Abbey, c 1375; Topcliffe near Thirsk, Yorkshire, 1391; and All Saints, Newcastle, 1411. All except that to the Abbot at St Albans are to rich merchants. The largest is the earlier King's Lynn brass, 118 in (3 m) long, while the most elaborate is at Newark, with thirty-nine attendant figures. All are rather worn and so large that it is impracticable to illustrate them. The King's Lynn brasses have scenes at the bottom, one showing a peacock feast, and all are crowded with saints, angels, prophets and weepers. Every available space is used for decoration and as a result the figures are rather lost, unlike English brasses where the opposite is the case. Later Flemish brasses, in fact, are even worse in this respect, for insofar as the fourteenth-century figures stand out at all it is because they are plainly dressed, but on the later brasses the figures have embroidered clothes that merge completely with the background.

Two smaller Flemish brasses that are very similar in design are to be found at North Mimms near Hatfield, Hertfordshire, c 1370, and Wensley, Yorkshire, c 1375. Both show priests in Mass vestments with chalices, the North Mimms brass including a canopy with saints. They are identifiable as Flemish by the style of their engraving and the very elaborate orphreys on the vestments, but both are cut out and set into stones in the English fashion. There is, however, some doubt whether the North Mimms one was not originally rectangular and later cut out to suit the English taste.

After about 1425 there are no more huge brasses that have survived, though there is an enormous Flemish incised slab at East Horndon, Essex, dated 1422 but engraved c 1440. Later Flemish brasses are to be found in Ipswich Museum, 1525 (formerly in St Mary Quay, Ipswich), and All Hallows Barking, London, 1533; they are small and very similar plates to merchants and their families. An attractive little lozenge-shaped brass survives at Fulham, London, 1529, to Margaret Svanders, the wife of Gerard Hornebolt, 'a most renowned painter from Ghent'. Gerard, in fact, was an obscure painter, but he probably designed the brass (Fig 71).

There are several good Flemish incised slabs left in Scotland; and one fine brass, in St Nicholas church, Aberdeen, 1613, showing a professor in his study surrounded by his books, very much in the style of contemporary portraits. It was made by Gaspard Bruydegoms of the Antwerp mint, and cost £87 10s 6d Flemish (see p 30).

There are few French brasses in England and the most important are by the banks of the Thames Estuary, near their ports of importation: two may be found at Minster-in-Sheppey, Kent, c 1330 and c 1335, and one at Aveley, Essex, c 1370. The Minster brasses (Fig 72) commemorate a knight and a lady, though there is no evidence that they were husband and wife and they are in fact usually dated five years apart. Their chief peculiarity is their costume, particularly that of the knight, which illustrates the foreign custom of wearing the shield at the hip. The lower part of his figure is a clumsy restoration (see p 58).

The Aveley brass, also to a knight, is usually considered Flemish, but its simplicity and general design is much closer to some French incised slabs than to Flemish work. It is engraved on a very small rectangular plate, with a simple canopy, and has a feature now unique in England—the jupon is omitted and the brigandine (the metal defence usually concealed by the jupon) exposed. Sword and dagger are attached by chains to the brigandine.

In addition to imported brasses there are several that show signs of foreign influence, though not enough to justify including them among

*Fig 71.*  Margaret Svanders, 1529, Fulham,
London

*Fig 72.*  (?) Sir John de Northwood, c 1330,
Minster-in-Sheppey, Kent

imported brasses. The knight at Chartham near Canterbury, 1306, and a priest at Horsmonden near Tunbridge Wells, c 1340, both in Kent, may have been designed in imitation of foreign work, probably French, or they may be the work of an immigrant engraver. The great brass to Sir Hugh Hastings from Elsing, Norfolk, 1347 (Fig 31), is usually described as influenced by Flemish design, or even actually imported, though it is probably English since the side-figures are so very close in design to English embroidery (cf page 133), and it is laid in English stone.

The great revival of brass-engraving in the late-sixteenth century was partly inspired by refugees from Flanders, but they brought with them not so much style as ability.

The greatest amount of foreign brass in England, again mostly Flemish, is found on the backs of palimpsests of the sixteenth century, as has already been described (see p 56). These are, however, only mutilated fragments and even when several palimpsests can be fitted together there is never enough to reconstruct more than parts of a brass, and it is unlikely that a complete brass will ever be made up from palimpsest fragments.

A few foreign brasses have somehow found their way into museums in England, the most important being the Flemish head of a bishop under a canopy, c 1380, and an elaborate Crucifixion, 1547, from Jeumont in France, both in the British Museum. There is also a rectangular plate from Watton, near Furnes, Belgium, 1504, and a beautiful little brass showing the Virgin and Child, St Peter and St Henry, from Nippes near Cologne, 1535, both of which are in the Victoria and Albert Museum, London.

The reverse of this importation of foreign brasses into England can be seen in the fragments of English brasses remaining in the areas of France formerly under English rule, such as Bordeaux, and the fine canopied brass to Robert Hallum, Bishop of Salisbury, who died during the Council of Constance in 1417, and was buried in Constance Cathedral, Germany.

H

# 6 ✤ Heraldry, Architecture, Symbols and Inscriptions

ARMORIAL BEARINGS ARE included in the composition of a great many, possibly the majority of, brasses and to appreciate these fully it is necessary to know something of the science of heraldry. Brasses that have lost their inscriptions can be identified and family connections traced. There are many good books on the subject, so it is just touched on here.

During the battle of Hastings a rumour spread that Duke William had been killed, and to check this he had to take off his helmet to identify himself. Obviously such action was inconvenient and dangerous, and consequently the custom arose and spread of painting badges on the knights' shields. The earliest devices were simple and easy to recognise, frequently an animal, sometimes punning on the knight's name, as the bear for FitzUrse, or merely a strengthening bar on the shield painted a different colour. Originally there was no family significance, and a knight's son could bear a completely different shield from that of his father. A knight's followers and retainers often bore his device, distinguished by some minor alteration. Later, however, arms became, as they still remain, strictly hereditary.

It eventually became obvious that some sort of registration would have to be made of these devices to prevent duplication, and so around the mid-fourteenth century the king assumed complete control over all armorial bearings. He alone could authorise their use and settle disputes over their ownership. This power was delegated to the officers of arms, namely the pursuivants, heralds and kings of arms, under the earl marshal, who granted and recorded all coats-of-arms and ensured that only the worthy might bear them. No brass, unfortunately, has survived to an officer of arms, but a herald in his heraldic tabard is shown on an allegorical design at Broughton Gifford near Melksham, Wiltshire.

Describing, or *blazoning* a coat-of-arms depends on rigid formulas and conventions, and is done in technical terms, most of which are of French origin but pronounced as if they were English. But once the 'language of heraldry' has been learnt, it is easy to describe any coat-of-arms quickly and precisely.

Positions on a shield are always described as *dexter* and *sinister*, that is right and left as the knight holding the shield sees it, or reversed as we look at it. The same terms are used in describing the position of a shield on a brass. The main *tinctures* used in heraldry are of two kinds: metals, *or* (gold) and *argent* (silver); and colours, *gules* (red), *azure* (blue), *sable* (black) and *vert* (green), as well as the furs, *ermine*, represented as silver with black tails or 'spots', and *vair*, alternate patches of blue and silver. The tinctures in heraldry are always kept distinct, metal never touching metal nor colour touching colour, since gold and silver tend to merge together and, to a lesser extent, so do red, blue, green and black. The same principle is followed on most national flags.

The charges on a shield are either 'ordinary' or 'common', the ordinaries being those formed by painting the construction bars of a shield. These ordinary charges form the *chief* along the top edge, the *fess* across the middle, the *pale* down the middle, together forming the *cross*; the *bend*,

*Fig 73.* Heraldic Details: (a) Camoys, within a Garter, (b) Covert, (c) Hailsham, (d) Wyvil, (e) Culpeper, (f) Andrewe, (g) Cobham, (h) Barttelot quartering Stopham, (i) Barttelot with many quarters, (j) Camoys impaling Mortimer (k) Canterbury impaling Laud, (l) Lozenge of Culpeper, (m) Crest of Drayton, (n) Crest of Hauberk

diagonally to the top dexter corner, very rarely the *bend sinister*, diagonally opposite, together forming the *saltire* or St Andrew's cross; and the *chevron*, originally two diagonals meeting in the middle of the top but later debased to a bent fess. These can be combined or duplicated, studded with *roundels* to represent nail heads, surcharged with other devices, or diminished. Illustrations are given of most of these ordinaries (Fig 73). Common charges are anything—animal, vegetable, mineral or imaginary, often forming a pun on the family name—and these can be entire, cut or torn apart, half covered by another charge, in any colour or in their natural colours (described as 'proper'). The lion is by far the favourite, and can be shown in a great many positions such as *rampant*, on its hind legs in attack, or *couchant*, asleep.

The shield of arms can be *differenced* by the addition of certain small marks to distinguish between the various branches of a family. Although some families altered their coat-of-arms completely, such as the lions of Cobham replaced by eagles or stars in lateral branches, most used the normal *cadency* marks. The most conspicuous of these marks is the *label*, the mark of an eldest son, formed by a narrow band across the top of the shield with three or five pendants from it, as on the shield of Bowthe at East Horsley near Guildford (Fig 25).

Normally only the shield appears on a brass, either as part of a large design or with no more than an inscription. The earliest shields were nearly triangular, but soon became elongated and, when a very complicated coat-of-arms had to be shown, almost square. A few late shields are cut and scalloped into scroll-forms.

The earliest brasses date from before the time when heraldry was regulated and the charges are very simple with no elaborate distinctions. Sir John Daubernoun merely bears two reinforcing bars painted gold; Sir Roger de Trumpington has trumpets and several small crosses which may or may not have anything to do with the fact that he was a crusader; Sir Robert de Septvans has winnowing fans (Fig 4).

A man who owned a coat-of-arms was known as an *armiger* or esquire, and when he married the arms of his wife were combined with his. If she was an heiress and brought in property, that is if she had no brothers, they were permanently united by *quartering*, dividing the shield into four and alternating the two coats-of-arms, as in the union of Barttelot with Stopham (Fig 73h). Successive marriages among descendants could lead to very elaborate coats-of-arms with many 'quarters' (Fig 73i). When, however, a wife was not an heiress, her arms were *impaled* with those of her husband, appearing on the sinister half of his shield as in the marriage of Camoys with Mortimer (Fig 73j), in which case the children bore only their father's

*Fig 74.* Henry Barttelot, 1710, Stopham, Sussex

*Fig 75.* Sir John de Wingfield, 1389, Leatheringham, Suffolk

arms. A bishop was considered to be married to his diocese, and so the diocesan arms were impaled with his, as in Canterbury impaling Laud (Fig 73k). Technically women were not supposed to carry shields, and displayed their arms on a *lozenge* or diamond-shape (Fig 73*l*), but in fact nearly all brasses of women display shields.

The other important part of a coat-of-arms is the *crest*, which served like the shield to identify a knight, though more in the tournament than in battle. The crest was made of wood or boiled leather and was fixed to the top of the jousting-helm, the join being covered by a wreath. It frequently took the form of an animal or a hand grasping a weapon but many other devices were used, such as the Saracen's head (Fig 73m). Helmets with their crests are often used as pillows on brasses, as with Nicholas Hauberk and his crest of a fish (Fig 73n).

The helmet is usually shown with a cloth or *mantling* hanging from it. This was originally a practical garment like the surcoat, designed to keep the sun off the helmet and prevent the knight from being boiled in his shell. Later it became a mere ornament and is shown cut and twisted into most elaborate designs, especially when the coat-of-arms is shown as a separate entity, as on the fine late brass to Henry Barttelot of Stopham (Fig 74). The space below the shield on such a coat-of-arms or *achievement* is frequently occupied by a scroll bearing a motto or war cry, often a pun on the family name such as the famous 'Festina Lente' for Onslow. Sometimes, the shield is held up by *supporters*, that is animals or figures on each side, a practice usually confined to the arms of the nobility. The shield may be encircled by the Garter or some chain of office or dignity, as on the Camoys shield (Fig 73a). Occasionally it is surrounded by a wreath to imitate these honours.

A few brasses show banners instead of shields, as at Lingfield and Ashford (Figs 12, 79). A very rare form of heraldic brass was formerly to be seen at Lytchett Matravers near Poole, Dorset, where the arms of John Matravers, one of the assassins of Edward II, were represented by an enormous black stone with an interlacing trellis of strips of brass, to represent 'sable, fretty or'. Unfortunately the brass is now lost except for a fragment of the marginal inscription, but the indents remain clear.

Coats-of-arms were frequently shown embroidered on clothes, as has been said. The earliest of such brasses, showing heraldic surcoats or jupons, as at Leatheringham near Wickham Market, Suffolk (Fig 75), usually bear only one coat-of-arms, but sixteenth-century tabards and mantles have as many quarterings as can be fitted in. There are a great number on the tabard already mentioned at Burton near Petworth, Sussex (Fig 56). The frontispiece shows part of Sir Thomas Bullen's heraldic tabard appearing below his Garter robes and bearing the Bullen arms 'party per fess indented azure and or' (divided into two colours by a zig-zag or *indented* line). The crest, 'a demi-eagle argent', appears on his helmet.

Heraldic badges, either single charges taken out of the shield or a completely separate device such as the chained swan of Gloucester (Fig 11), are sometimes found worked into the design of a canopy or cope, used to space the words of an inscription or scattered all over the surface of the stone. Heraldic animals are also sometimes placed beneath a figure's feet, such as a leopard at Digswell near Welwyn, Hertfordshire; a unicorn at Ewelme near Dorchester, Oxfordshire; or eagles at Little Easton near Dunmow, Essex.

During the Middle Ages only military families were entitled to coats-of-arms, so the rich merchants displayed *merchant's marks* instead. These

*Fig 76.* Merchants' Marks: (a) Dorchester, Oxford-shire, (b) Hereford Cathedral, (c) Hawkhurst, Kent, (d) Cranbrook, Kent (e) Orford, Suffolk

were trademarks used to brand goods for identification, some being of very ancient origin, derived from runes and usually Christianised with a cross. Successive branches of a family added to these marks and some became very complicated. They were not recognised as heraldic, though their purpose was the same, and the heralds had power to erase them if they were shown on shields. Nevertheless a great many such marks are shown on shields, as in the examples illustrated (Fig 76), though some conformed to the law and appeared on square or round plates. They were frequently combined with initials, as on three of the examples shown. These marks are sometimes shown on brasses as branded on woolsacks beneath the feet of wool merchants and in one case enclosed within elaborate wreaths of ivy. Many tradesmen and merchants display the arms of the company or guild to which they belonged, as did Robert Chapman of Stone, near Dartford, Kent, who, besides his own arms, bears the arms of the Merchant Venturers and the Drapers' Company (Fig 77).

Another type of device related to heraldry is the *rebus* or punning object, which is very similar to punning coats-of-arms, which have already been mentioned, and was derived from them. An early example is the brass of Margarete de Camoys, whose slab was strewn with daisies or *marguerites* (Fig 9). Others are the barrel or *tun* on brasses to John Stock-ton in Hereford Cathedral and to Robert Lang-ton in The Queen's College, Oxford, a goose for John Goose at East Dereham, Norfolk, and a rose for Rose

*Fig 77.*   Robert Chapman, 1574, Stone, Kent

Glover at Shottisham near Woodbridge, Suffolk. They were very popular,
specially during the sixteenth century, and in an age when few could read
conveyed the names of the dead to a far wider range of people than
inscriptions could alone.

### ARCHITECTURE ON BRASSES

Several of the finest medieval brasses show figures under canopies, and
the latter were usually designed in the style of contemporary ecclesiastical
architecture. After the Renaissance canopies are no longer found but the
background to brasses is very often an architectural structure, sometimes of
considerable interest.

Canopied brasses were naturally among the most expensive and so were

*Fig 78.* Lady, c 1420,
Horley, Surrey

*Fig 79.* Eleanor Cobham,
1420, Lingfield, Surrey

chiefly laid in the churches of large towns and cities that have been the most plundered. As a result good canopies are rare on brasses but representative examples of all types survive. By their nature also they leave very distinct indents, so many details are known of lost canopies.

The medieval type of canopy consisted basically of two shafts supporting an arch and rising into pinnacles, as on the brass to an unknown woman at Horley, Surrey, c 1420 (Fig 78). This type of canopy derives from the solid canopies on three-dimensional tombs, which enclose the figure, as do those of Edward III and Richard II in Westminster Abbey; and the solid canopies are in turn derived from stone arches erected over tombs, specially those set into the wall. In all cases the canopy is designed as a mark of honour, protecting the figure below, its splendour and size increasing with the status—or more often the ostentation—of the person commemorated by the tomb.

Canopies appeared on the earliest brasses and incised slabs, as on the Wells Cathedral slab already mentioned (Fig 6). The earliest had straight-sided gables but only one example of this type survives in brass, at Cobham, Kent, c 1320; but the indents of others can be clearly seen, as on the Trotton brass described earlier (Fig 9), where the centres of the gable and cusps were cut away to show the stone.

The next surviving canopy, that of Sir John Daubernoun the Younger at Stoke D'Abernon near Cobham, Surrey (Fig 30), shows the ogee arch that superseded the straight-sided gable and is characteristic of nearly all canopies on brasses. This double-curved arch is rare in English architecture but is the most attractive way of putting a pinnacle on to an arch and making a high and slender point to the canopy.

Many different types of canopy are found from the mid-fourteenth century onwards. Where husband and wife are shown side-by-side the canopy is double, usually without a centre shaft, as on the Deerhurst brass (Fig 61); and more important people have triple canopies with three arches and pendants, as does the Duchess of Gloucester in Westminster Abbey (Fig 11). A sextuple canopy is even found occasionally, with husband and wife each under a triple arch. Side shafts of canopies can take a variety of forms: some are doubled, separated by niches containing figures of saints or weepers, each with its own little canopy; others are separated by arches and flying buttresses; some have shields hanging from the crockets of the pinnacles; and many have 'lancet windows', which were once filled with colour. Some of the finest canopies are surmounted by square-topped and battlemented super-canopies, and a few have further niches and yet another super-canopy. The Durham indent shows the clear outline of such a structure, with two rows of figures on each side, a triple ogee-canopy, a super-canopy and canopied niches above that. None of the English brasses, however, can match the splendour of Continental canopies, the greatest of which must be the incised slab in St Denis, Paris, with five rows of figures on each side and a total length of 7 metres.

As well as ogee-arched canopies there are a number of more individual designs, such as the rounded arches at Ashford, Kent (Fig 12), and Stoke Fleming near Dartmouth, Devonshire, or the square-topped canopy at Lingfield, Surrey (Fig 79). More elaborate and unusual canopies can be found on the brasses to Dean Frowcester, 1529, in Hereford Cathedral, which has 'onion-domes' like the Kremlin, and to Bishop Wyvil in Salisbury Cathedral, 1375, with the castle already described.

The design of the best canopies was 'Decorated' Gothic—slender, well proportioned, always striving upwards. After the middle of the fifteenth century, however, the design falls greatly in quality: the late Perpendicular style could not be translated into the traditional form, and the designs became clumsy and top-heavy imitations of earlier examples. Saints appear more frequently, and the fragments of the canopy of William Porter, 1524, in Hereford Cathedral (Fig 14) show the poor quality of the design— resplendent with saints and angels but clumsy and badly shaped, with appalling perspective. One of the chief faults of late canopies is the attempt at perspective, which was always unsuccessful, usually resulting in the canopy appearing twisted and precarious. The same failure attended the attempt to show groined vaults under the arches. It is not surprising that canopies died out altogether in the Renaissance.

Stylistically linked closely with canopies are brackets, which appear on a number of brasses from c 1340 onwards. In its purest form, as at Upper Hardres near Canterbury, 1405, the bracket has a straight shaft rising from steps and a splay at the top where stand the figures, usually the people commemorated but occasionally saints, as at Upper Hardres. Variations on this form are found with the stem footed on an animal, such as a fox on the Foxle brass at Bray near Maidenhead, Berkshire, or a tabernacle enclosing the Agnus Dei at Merton College, Oxford (Fig 63). Several brasses have or had canopies over the figures on top of the bracket, a fine little example being that to Reginald de Cobham, 1402, at Cobham, Kent (Fig 80). Fourteenth- and fifteenth-century brackets remain strictly archi- tectural, but later examples, such as one at St John Maddermarket, Norwich, 1524, are shaped like trees with figures standing on the branches. When perspective is introduced on brackets the result is even worse than on canopies—the top surface of the bracket usually looks as if it were falling forwards and it seems to have no connection with the figures. Another bracket-brass at St John Maddermarket, Norwich, shows the figures balanced on the corners of a bracket whose surface is strewn with bones. Brackets die out about the same time as canopies. They are a curious phenomenon and no really satisfactory explanation has been given for their origin, unless they derive from image-brackets, in which case it seems odd that the majority of those surviving should not show saints but the people commemorated, on top. Designed in very much the same way as brackets are *crosses*, about which more will be said in the section on symbolic representations below.

During the troubled years of the mid-sixteenth century, when brasses were few and bad, no canopies or other architectural details appear on them, and in the revival of brass-engraving the ideal of the effigy under a canopy was abandoned completely in favour of kneeling figures against a background of classical architecture, as on the Shepton Mallet brass (Fig 17). The backgrounds are usually restrained, in order to add interest to the composition but not to overpower it as some medieval canopies did. The architecture is at first correctly classical but later it breaks out into Baroque. Some of the more elaborate pictorial brasses show complete buildings, as on Bishop Robinson's brass in The Queen's College, Oxford (Fig 26) with Carlisle Cathedral and the college as it was in his time. Other brasses restrict their architectural detail to frames, an unusual example of which can be seen at Colemore near Petersfield, Hampshire, 1641 (Fig 81). Its design clearly imitates the marble architectural frames round so many contemporary wall-plaques, typical of Baroque architecture with scrolls and broken pediments.

Victorian brasses, needless to say, show canopies of Gothic design, usually rather bad imitations of fourteenth-century examples. There are several in Westminster Abbey.

### SYMBOLIC REPRESENTATIONS ON BRASSES

Many brasses from all periods include in the design some symbolic or allegorical feature, usually with a religious significance, which are often of great interest and sometimes artistically important. Before the Reformation, symbols and straight-forward representations of religious subjects were common, though comparatively few have survived; later the preference was for more obscure allegorical motifs.

The most elaborate of the medieval religious representations were the scenes from the life of Christ which were usually worked into the design of a canopy. The Annunciation is fairly common, particularly in the West of England, and there are fragments of two at Cirencester, a fine little one with the figure of the man commemorated included in it at Fovant near Salisbury, and the large one at Hereford already described (Fig 14). All showed, when complete, the Angel Gabriel appearing to the Virgin, a pot of lilies and the Holy Ghost descending in the form of a dove. The words of salutation are given on scrolls: *Ave gratia plena dominus tecum*—'Hail, full of grace, the Lord is with thee', spoken by the angel; and Mary's answer, *Ecce ancilla domini fiat mihi secundum verbum tuum*—'Behold the handmaid of the Lord, be it done unto me according to thy word', which, as it is addressed to Heaven, is written upside down.

Fig 81. John and Sarah Greaves, 1541, Colemore, Hampshire

Fig 80. Reginald de Cobham, 1402, Cobham,
Kent

The Adoration of the Shepherds appears on a curious little brass at Cobham, Surrey, c 1500, where the scene is dominated by a large head, apparently St Joseph's. The Virgin and Child are shown on a great many brasses, some of the figures being very beautiful. Examples may be seen at Cobham, Kent and Cowfold, Sussex (Fig 82a).

The Crucifixion was formerly shown on several brasses, but these particularly aroused the hatred of the Reformers and only one remains complete, at Kenton near Debenham, Suffolk. There are also fragments at Chelsfield near Orpington, South London. The Instruments of the Passion survive on a few brasses, as at St Cross, Winchester, where they are shown on a shield (Fig 82b). A few modern brasses, as in the Catholic church at Petworth, Sussex, show Crucifixions. The Pietà, the Virgin mourning over the dead Christ, appears on a canopy at Carshalton, South London (Fig 82c). The Resurrection is more frequently found, as might be expected on a tomb, and invariably shows Christ stepping triumphantly out of an altar-tomb surrounded by sleeping soldiers, as at Slaugham near Crawley, Sussex (Fig 82d). Christ in Glory is shown at Mereworth near Wrotham, Kent, and a fragment of the Ascension nearby at Ightham. The Holy Trinity is perhaps the most frequent of all, usually showing God the Father seated on a throne and holding His Crucified Son on His knees, while the Holy Ghost flies between them; there is a fine example at Cobham, Kent

*Fig 82.* Religious Scenes: (a) Virgin and Child, Cowfold, Sussex, (b) Instruments of the Passion, St Cross, Winchester, (c) Pietá, Carshalton, London, (d) Resurrection, Slaugham, Sussex, (e) Trinity, Cobham, Kent, (f) Verbal Trinity, Cowfold, Sussex

*Fig 83.* Nichol de Gore, 1333,
Woodchurch, Kent

*Fig 84.* Richard Tooner, 1445,
Broadwater, Sussex

(Fig 82e). An alternative form of the Trinity was the 'verbal symbol', a diagram usually shown on a shield, as at Cowfold, Sussex (Fig 82f).

An unusual brass at Macclesfield, Cheshire, shows the 'Mass of St Gregory', with the risen Christ appearing to St Gregory while he is saying Mass. This design is apparently based on a confusion of three stories from the *Dialogues of St Gregory* and the *Golden Legend*—first, the story of a monk who had been excommunicated by St Gregory and after his death appeared to the saint during Mass; second, the story that once while giving Communion St Gregory saw the Host as the bleeding flesh of Christ; and third, the story that an angel once served Mass for St Gregory.

Although only one complete crucifix survives on a brass in England, there are a great many crosses, which, as already stated, were among the earliest brass designs, appearing in Westminster Abbey in 1276, and 1277. The earliest of which any substantial part survives is in Merton College Chapel, Oxford, 1311, where the half-effigy of a priest is shown in the head of a large floriated cross. This position for a figure was very common and not only half-effigies but full length and even pairs of effigies are found, as at Woodchurch near Tenterden, Kent (Fig 83), and Wimbish near Halstead, Essex (page 49).

The arms of the cross usually end in leaves or fleur-de-lys, and the circle enclosing the figure may be cusped, as at Woodchurch, or broken up into four or eight arches, as at Wimbish (page 49) or Stone near Dartford, Kent. This circle could be inscribed as also could the stem or base of the cross. Usually this base was a flight of steps but, as at the base of a bracket, animals or other objects could be placed there, like the elephant formerly on the Wimbish cross.

A few brasses show figures kneeling at the foot of a cross, while a saint, as at Newton by Geddington, Northamptonshire, or a Trinity, as at Hildersham near Cambridge, is enclosed in the head. An unusual cross at Higham Ferrers near Northampton shows the Resurrection in the centre and the Evangelistic symbols at the ends of the arms.

Crosses without figures were less common but there are several impressive examples, such as that at Grainthorpe near Grimsby, Lincolnshire, or Broadwater near Worthing, Sussex (Fig 84), where the arms are inscribed with verses from the *Anima Christi*. Two very small crosses at Hever and Penshurst near Tonbridge, Kent, are completely plain, but both have been restored and may originally have been crucifixes. Also at Hever is a palimpsest fragment of a cross lined to represent wood, with the Five Wounds in the centre, and the Five Wounds also appear clearly on an indent for a cross in St Andrews, Norwich.

Cross brasses were among those most hated by the Reformers, and so it is hardly surprising that the series came to an end in the mid-sixteenth century, apart from a few very small and modest plain crosses during the seventeenth century. The nineteenth century revived cross brasses and they became very common. One of the most elaborate is in Westminster Abbey and shows Sir Charles Barry kneeling at the foot of a cross beside which are the Tower of the House of Lords and the plan of Westminster Palace.

Figures of saints survive on many fewer brasses than do crosses or religious scenes, and where they do survive they are usually in groups. As already mentioned they appear mostly in the shafts of canopies or the orphreys of copes, each in a separate niche and often with the name under-

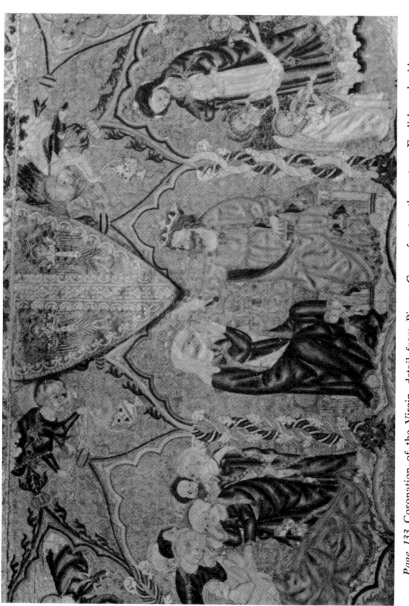

*Page 133* Coronation of the Virgin, detail from Pienza Cope, fourteenth century English embroidery

*Page 134* Detail of tomb of William de Valence, 1296, Westminster Abbey

neath. A wide range of saints, biblical and historical, is shown, and some of them, like St Sythe or sometimes Osyth at Tattershall, Lincolnshire, are very obscure. The Virgin Mary is the most popular saint, usually holding the Child Jesus but occasionally being taught to read by her mother, St Anne, as at Deerhurst near Tewkesbury, Gloucestershire (Fig 85b), or being crowned Queen of Heaven, as at Elsing near East Dereham, Norfolk (Fig 85a).

The Twelve Apostles, Paul taking the place of Judas, appear together on some brasses and individual apostles on several more, SS Peter and Paul being the most frequent, as at Upper Hardres near Canterbury. The next most popular are Christopher carrying Christ through the river, as at Weeke near Winchester (Fig 85c) and George and his Dragon, as at Cobham, Kent (Fig 85d). St Thomas of Canterbury is also common, as at Cowfold, Sussex (Fig 85e). He has been replaced in Hereford Cathedral by St Thomas of Hereford, whose story has already been told. Other local saints are SS Richard, Wilfred, Ethelbert (Fig 7), Edmund, Osyth and David, and formerly SS Alban and Amphibalus. St John the Baptist appears fairly

*Fig 85.* Saints: (a) Coronation of the Virgin, Elsing, Norfolk, (b) SS Anne and Mary, Deerhurst, Gloucestershire, (c) St Christopher, Weeke, Hampshire, (d) St George, Cobham, Kent, (e) St Thomas, Cowfold, Sussex, (f) Evangelistic Symbols, Seal, Kent

I

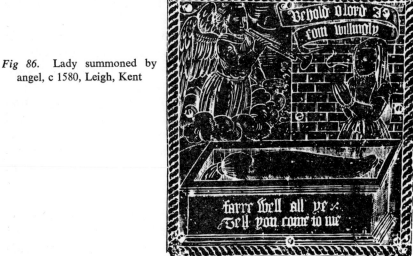

*Fig 86.* Lady summoned by
angel, c 1580, Leigh, Kent

*Fig 87.* Roses: (a) from canopy, West Grinstead,
Sussex, (b) from canopy, Hereford Cathedral, (c) Symbol
of St Mark, Ely Cathedral, (d) Littleton, Surrey

frequently, the scene of his beheading being shown at Hereford; while Mary Magdalen, Katherine and Michael weighing souls appear a few times. Many of the saints have their special attributes, such as St Peter's keys and St Katherine's wheel, by which they can easily be recognised.

The most frequent of all are Matthew, Mark, Luke and John, usually shown not in human form but by the mystical symbols of angel, lion, ox and eagle. They appear at the angles of marginal inscriptions and often at the corners of a slab even if there is no inscription (Fig 85f). An unusually late example appears on the brass to Archbishop Harsnett, 1631 (Fig 1) where the four are shown in human form but with their mystical symbols beside them.

Angels often appear on elaborate brasses, either swinging censers to the main effigy or to a Trinity, or holding up a pillow beneath the main figure's head, as at Hever, Kent. On a few brasses, as at Elsing, Norfolk, the angels are holding a sheet in which the soul of the dead man, represented as a naked figure, is carried up to heaven; and on others they appear sounding the Last Trump and arousing the dead, as at Leigh near Tonbridge, Kent (Fig 86). Angels alone among religious symbols were acceptable to the Reformers and are shown on quite late brasses, though winged heads are more common in the eighteenth century.

In addition to patent religious representations a great many brasses show less obvious symbols. Of these by far the most common are flowers, with the almost universal use of the rose. The rose is a very ancient symbol of love and is used on brasses as symbolic both of the love of God through which men hope to be saved, and, more frequently, of the Virgin Mary. However, the natural form of the rose was not sufficient: the medieval obsession with symmetry demanded that it have four petals (not five) whose conjunction of the sepals thus made a cross, neatly combining the two symbols (Fig 87a). During the Renaissance desire for naturalism overcame symbolism, and the rose is shown properly with five petals (Fig 87b). The rose appears on orphreys of copes and chasubles, and worked into the design of canopies on hundreds of brasses. It is commonly the central feature of the gable and cusps of canopies, where it is sometimes reduced to three rose-leaves to fit the triangular space and, incidentally, symbolise the Trinity. Evangelistic symbols are usually shown on plates the shape of a four-petalled rose, though at Ely Cathedral the rose is drawn round the symbols (Fig 87c). At Ashford, Kent, there is a wreath of roses enclosing an inscription, and large inscribed roses appear at Littleton near Staines (Fig 87d), Mawgan-in-Pyder, Cornwall and Edlesborough, Buckinghamshire. An enormous rose with inscription and scrolls, which was formerly in Westminster Abbey, is illustrated in Richard Gough's *Sepulchral Monu-*

*ments* (vol II, 210). The rosary is sometimes shown hanging from a belt with a clasp of three roses, as at St Helen's Bishopsgate, London (Fig 55).

Many late brasses show figures holding roses, which are drawn completely naturally, as at Wooburn, Buckinghamshire. The three daughters of Nicholas Toke from Great Chart near Ashford, Kent, 1680, hold a rose, a palm branch and an olive branch respectively, as symbols of love, triumph and peace (Fig 21). The rose also appears as a rebus on the brass to Rose Glover, as already mentioned. The rose was also adopted as a political symbol, of course, and its appearance is political rather than religious on brasses to supporters of the York, Lancaster and Tudor houses.

Other flower symbols are lilies for purity, shown naturally in Annunciations but stylised into the fleur-de-lys on many brasses, particularly as the finials to crosses; and trefoils for the Trinity, growing at the feet of some figures. A tree, as Tree of Life or Tree of Knowledge, is shown on a few brasses, as at St John Maddermarket, Norwich.

Animal symbols are more varied but less common than flowers and it is often difficult to sort out purely symbolic from heraldic animals. The lion for courage and the hound for manly sport have already been mentioned as appearing at the feet of military effigies. The lap-dog, usually with a collar of bells, is often shown at the feet of women as a symbol of fidelity, though one called Terri, whose name is inscribed on the Cassy brass at Deerhurst, Gloucestershire (Fig 61), was clearly a favourite pet. The crane appears as a symbol of watchfulness at Old Buckenham near Norwich (Fig 88b) and as part of Bishop Robinson's brass from The Queen's College, Oxford (Fig 26). The crane was believed to keep watch with a stone held in its claws, so that the stone would drop and wake it up if it fell asleep. Margaret Willoughby of Raveningham, Norfolk, near Beccles, has a dragon, the attribute of St Margaret, at her feet; and a lady at Digswell, Hertfordshire, has a swan embroidered on her collar and a hedgehog at her feet. Small figures of animals or plants are often worked into brass inscriptions as stops between words, particularly in the West of England, and there is a good series at Northleach (Fig 88a), including a slug; but these figures are more decorative than symbolic. Two little animals at Charwelton near Daventry, Northamptonshire (Fig 88c), however, are probably symbolic—a dog eating out of a cauldron representing home and security and a dragon standing for the wildness and danger of life outside.

The Pelican-in-her-Piety appears on a canopy at Warbleton near Heathfield, Sussex (Fig 88d). The pelican was believed to feed her young with her own blood and is consequently a symbol of charity and the love of God. The Agnus Dei that supports the bracket-brass at Merton College, Oxford (Fig 63), is a more familiar symbol. Many other animals are found on

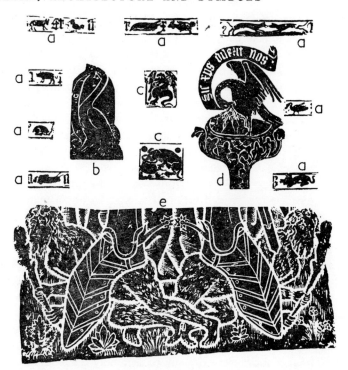

*Fig 88.* Animals: (a) details from inscription, Northleach, Gloucestershire, (b) Crane, Old Buckenham, Norfolk, (c) Dragon and Dog, Charwelton, Northamptonshire, (d) Pelican, Warbleton, Sussex (e) Woodhouses, Tattershall, Lincolnshire

brasses, some as symbols, some as trade emblems (such as sheep for wool merchants), and some as punning rebuses. At St Mary-the-Great, Cambridge praising God *voce et odore* 'by voice and sweet savour' is represented by flowers and a song thrush.

A curious apparition on a few brasses is the Woodhouse or Hairy Man, a sort of Abominable Snowman believed to lurk in the forests of central Europe. It appears chiefly on foreign brasses but is also shown on English work at Tattershall, Lincolnshire (Fig 88e), and Holwell, Bedfordshire, near Letchworth.

The fylvot or swastika is worked into the orphreys of vestments on a great many brasses. Originally an Indian symbol, by the Middle Ages it had become quite meaningless and is used indiscriminately facing left or right.

Several seventeenth- and eighteenth-century brasses have rather obscure allegorical designs or emblems typical of the time—the visual equivalent of

Bunyan's *Pilgrim's Progress*. The most elaborate are those designed by Richard Haydock and already described, but many lesser examples occur. The incised slab from Cuckfield, Sussex (Fig 19), which is almost certainly by Epiphany Evesham, shows six little emblems each neatly illustrating a motto or phrase from the scriptures. The most common allegorical designs are the emblems of mortality, the 'graves, worms and epitaphs' already mentioned. Death frequently appears in his character of unwelcome guest, announcing his unexpected presence with a dart. On a brass at Biggleswade, Bedfordshire, the inscription includes a dialogue between the reader and Death, who points his dart at what he is saying.

A curious late allegorical brass from Malton in the North Riding of Yorkshire shows a plate divided into two scenes: in one a man is praying devoutly, while in the other he is having a wild drinking party and waving a bottle. The inscription says: 'Here lies one when living Had his virtues and his vices: Copy his virtues & shun his vices. Arthur Gibson, Whitesmith, Brass and Iron Founder, Ob$^t$ 20 August 1837, at Malton. Aged 74'. Presumably the brass was made in his own foundry in accordance with his instructions.

Less ambitious emblems occur frequently, several brasses showing hearts and palm branches. Hearts also appear on a number of brasses with a meaning not allegorical but quite literal: they signify the separate burial of the heart. It is an ancient practice still occasionally used—Thomas Hardy, for example—to separate the heart from the body and bury it in some place specially loved by the person while alive. The heart is frequently shown on brasses by itself, with scrolls issuing from it, as at Margate, Kent, or held by two hands issuing from clouds, as in Chichester Cathedral. Usually the heart has the sacred monogram IHS or the word 'Credo' engraved on it. An unusual heart-monument, also in Chichester Cathedral and believed to commemorate Maud de Warenne, 1236, consisted of two hands holding the heart within a trefoil, all carved in the stone, and an inscription in separate brass letters round the edge. Unfortunately the brass is now lost and the stone too worn to read more than a few letters of the inscription. Other heart brasses show full length effigies holding the heart, indicating either a heart burial or merely a way of showing the man's faith to be so great that 'Credo' or 'Jesus' is engraved on his heart. Examples occur at Aldborough near Boroughbridge, Yorkshire; Graveney near Faversham, Kent; and St Albans Abbey, where the heart is shown bleeding (Fig 46).

A purely secular symbol on brasses is the trade symbol. It has already been mentioned that many tradesmen are shown on brasses with the instruments or products of their trade, or the animals connected with it;

*Fig 89.* Peter Denot, c 1450,
Fletching, Sussex

HERE LYFTH INTERRED THE BODY OF ROGER
MORRIS SOMETIME ONF OF THE 6 PRINCIPALL
M: OF ATTENDANCE OF HIS MA:- NAVYE
ROYALL WHO DEPARTED THIS LYFE THE
13 OF OCTOBER 1615

*Fig 90.* Roger Morris,
1615, Margate, Kent

but these symbols can also appear by themselves. Thus at Fletching near
Uckfield, Sussex, Peter Denot, glover, who was nearly hanged for taking
part in Jack Cade's revolt in 1450, is commemorated by a pair of gloves
(Fig 89). At St Mary-le-Wigford, Lincoln, a fishmonger has an axe and a
cleaver on his inscription; there is a hunting horn at Bexley, South London;
and a ship in full sail at Margate, Kent, commemorating 'one of the 6
Principall Masters of attendance of his Majesties Navye Royall' (Fig 90).
The chalice, as already mentioned, is a common symbol for priests, pre-
Reformation abbots and bishops were often commemorated by a crozier,
though none survive in brass, and later bishops were identified by a mitre.

Symbolism on brasses still needs a lot of study. Symbols were plentifully
used to instruct the illiterate, and as such are found in almost every branch
of medieval and Renaissance art.

### INSCRIPTIONS

It is the inscriptions that give real meaning to a brass. There are plenty of them to study, for most brasses in England never consisted of more than an inscription and perhaps a shield, and the figure brasses generally retain their inscriptions. Brasses cover every possible rank and profession from duchess to small farmer, and every date from 1276 to 1968 (both represented in Westminster Abbey).

Inscriptions are usually placed (1) round the edge of the slab containing brasses, as a 'marginal inscription', or (2) on a plate at the foot of the figure (a 'foot inscription'). Sometimes more than one placing can be found on the same brass. Prayers are often written on scrolls issuing from the mouth or hands of a figure, and inscriptions can also be found in such odd positions as round the arch of a canopy, up the stem of a cross, or over the breast of a figure. Inscriptions without figures nearly always appear on rectangular plates, though there are a few marginal inscriptions by themselves. On some brasses the inscription or part of it is cut on to the stone.

The lettering of inscriptions may be daunting at first but with a little practice nearly all can be deciphered. The earliest brasses had inscriptions in 'Lombardic' characters, large separate capital letters, which are usually quite easy to read. They were either set as separate letters in the stone, as at Trotton (Fig 9), or engraved on a continuous fillet of brass, as at Woodchurch (Fig 83) or Pebmarsh (Fig 28). Even when they have been lost, 'separate letter' inscriptions can often be read from the indents, unless the stone is badly worn, and in fact very few letters remain of these inscriptions.

From about 1350 to about 1550, 'black-letter' was almost invariably used. This is similar to old German print, the letters reduced as far as possible to straight lines. The fourteenth-century black-letter is fairly rounded and well spaced, but the fifteenth-century letters are jammed closely together and formed as regularly as possible, without the variations in form needed to distinguish one from the other. It was at this time that the custom arose of putting a dot over an i to distinguish it from the otherwise identical strokes of m, n, u and v. One of the most difficult inscriptions is that of Dom Robert Beaunor of St Albans Abbey (Fig 46); such inscriptions can only be read by guesswork and a good knowledge of the language involved. Towards the end of the fifteenth century the lettering became much more legible and wider spaced, and Arabic numbers, though not quite in the form we are used to, appeared as an alternative to Roman. One of the earliest examples can be seen at Lullingstone, Kent, 1487 (Fig 36).

With the revival of classical learning, Roman capitals became almost universal. They are easy to read, though contractions, such as running together the letters in 'THE', may make some words obscure; and it is also sometimes confusing when U is written as V and J as I, in words like 'IVLY' (July). A cursive handwritten script appears in the eighteenth century as a more attractive but still legible alternative to Roman.

Where Greek is used on inscriptions it appears in either capital letters or a very difficult cursive script. Cursive Greek combines or alters letters in a way that is almost incomprehensible to one used to classical or modern Greek forms, but it is, fortunately, rarely used on brasses.

The language of the earliest inscriptions was Norman French, half-way from Latin to modern French. Peculiar words and spellings are found but with a knowledge of modern French most inscriptions can be made out. Some of the oddities in wording may be due to English engravers unused to French.

Latin was used on inscriptions to clergy from the earliest times and finally replaced French at the beginning of the fifteenth century. Medieval Latin contains many words and constructions not found in classical Latin, but as they are mostly borrowed from English, they are easy to understand. Unusual spellings occur, logical only if the Italian or ecclesiastical pronunciation is used: thus *ae* is nearly always written *e*, as in *secula*; *ti*, often *ci*, as in *gracia*; and *mihi* becomes *michi*. More puzzling are the abbreviations and technical words, some of the most common of which are given here:

*dñs, dñi*, etc: *dominus, domini*: Lord
*or' p' āiā*: *orate pro anima*: pray for the soul
*cui' āiē p'piciet' de'*: *cuius animae propicietur deus*: may God have
  mercy on his soul
*ob't ob'*: *obiit*: he died
*huj' eccli'e*: *huius ecclesiae*: of this church.
*A° dñi*: AD, *Anno Domini*
pos., p.: *posuit*: placed
M.P.: *moerens posuit*: sorrowfully placed
H.S.J. or H.S.E: *Hic sepultus jacet* or *est*: here is buried
M.S.: *memoriae sacrum*: sacred to the memory
*Miles*: knight
*Comes*: earl
*armiger*: esquire
*generosus*: gentleman

The most common abbreviations are those formed by omitting m or n and putting a stroke over the word, thus *āiā* for *anima*, soul, and *quōdā* for *quondam*, once. Endings of words are often left off, such as *ei'* for *eius*, his or her. Jesus is very often spelt *Jhesus*, shortened to *Jhš* or *Jhū*, owing to a confusion with the Greek letters *IHCOYC*, in which the 'H' is really an E. Christ is also abbreviated to *Xpṡ*, again from the Greek *XPICTOC*. After the Renaissance, Latin became more regular, less abbreviations were used and the style improved.

English first appears at the end of the fourteenth century, but does not become popular until a hundred years later, after which it gradually supersedes Latin altogether. The earliest English inscriptions, written soon after Chaucer had proved that the language could have a literary form, are reminiscent of the *Canterbury Tales*, with many obsolete words and spellings. Frequent use is made of the 'thorn' letter, representing *th* and usually shaped like a 'y' reversed. Only after capitals began to be used, when 'thorn' and Y took the same form, did the nonsensical use of Y for *th* appear, as in 'ye'. The spelling remained erratic up to the eighteenth century, but the language gradually developed until it is quite easy to understand, though unfamiliar words may still occur. Deviant spellings can give an interesting illustration of contemporary pronunciation, such as 'dafter' for 'daughter', proving that the 'gh' in 'daughter' was originally pronounced as in 'laughter'.

The few inscriptions in Greek, Hebrew and other languages are confined to quotations, mostly from the scriptures, and so are of no linguistic interest.

The earliest inscriptions are very brief, merely giving the name of the dead person and adding a prayer for his soul. After about 1350 the date was nearly always added. As time advanced, longer and longer inscriptions were composed, giving details of the person's life and character and including romantic elegies on death.

Probably the shortest complete inscription is just the name, 'Iohannes Daniel', from Acton near Long Melford, Suffolk. The longest is undoubtedly one from North Cadbury near Wincanton, Somerset, with ninety-six verses in English. Verses range from the worst sort of doggerel to finely polished poetry. A typical example of rustic verse occurs at Aldeburgh, Suffolk, c 1570:

> To you that lyfe posses great troubles do befall
> When we that slepe by Death do feele no harme at all.
> An honest life dothe bringe A joyfull Deathe at last,
> And Life agayne begins when Deathe is over past.
> My lovinge Foxe farewell God mayde the wt his grace
> Prepare thyselfe to come And I will give the place.
> My children all adewe And be right sure of this
> You shall be brought to Dust As Emme Foxe yoᵣ Mother is.

A rather better example may be seen at Graffham near Petworth, Sussex, to a mother and her daughter, 1691:

> Death, to make recompenc for what he'd Done
> In partinge two whose harts were joyn'd in one
> Att length the other tooke, and heere they ly
> Waiteinge the summons to Eternity.
> The indulgent mother first went to prepare
> A lodging for her daughter. She for feare
> Her duty should be censured for her stay
> Courted her grave and gently fled away.

The majority of English verses are, unfortunately, in the style of the first quoted, with monotonous beats and ballad metres. The exact metre and echoes of the words of the eighteenth-century ballad 'John Gilpin' appear at Stone near Dartford, Kent, 1574:

> Loe here he lyeth that earst did lyve and Roberte Chapman highte
> To prove, by gods eternall dome that deathe wyll have his righte
> Owner of Stone Castell true what tyme he livued was he
> Esquier and Marchante Venterer, of London Draper Free.
> His soule, wee hoope, in Heaven dothe reste thoughe carcas lye full lo
> Thus god appoints the rightteous Manne, A fynall ende of woe.
> Whose monumente alofte dothe stande for every man to viewe,
> Whereby wee learne what brittle steppes all Mortall men ensue.

Latin verse is usually written in hexameters or elegiacs of equally varying quality. One of the worst is that already quoted (p 14) from Findon near Worthing, Sussex. During the Middle Ages Latin verse was composed more by rhyme than metre, and may be twisted into the most awkward phrases to fit both. When the date is introduced chaos ensues, for instance at Faversham, Kent:

> *Aprilis deno luce cessit ab hac que kalendas*
> *Anno milleno quatuor cent' bis quat' addas/x.*

Literally, 'he departed from this light on the tenth day before the Kalends (new moon) of April in the year one thousand four hundred add twice four times ten', meaning 23 March 1480. Again at Stopham, Sussex:

> MD demetur X octo X̄p̄i ruit annus.

'Fifteen hundred, take away eighteen runs the year of Christ', meaning 1482.

The clumsy ancient Roman system of dating backwards from the new, quarter or full moon, is only used on verse inscriptions. Most are reasonable enough to use the day of the month. Later verses omit the date, which is put in prose as a postscript, and so are much easier to understand as well as being better verse. A curious example from Chichester Cathedral commemorating Henry Ball, Archdeacon, 1603, is constantly broken by sighs, as follows:

> *(Balle iaces) juste cunctis deflendus amicus*
> *Omnibus (heu) tristi funere (Balle iaces).*

*(Balle iaces) vitae cunctis exemplar honestae*
*Dulcisonans verbi Buccina: (Balle iaces).*
*Pauperibus pater: Aegrotis solamen: et istis*
*Aedibus (ah), merito gloria: (Balle iaces).*
*Dilecti quondam Biclaei praesulis ossa*
*Iuxta, hic contiguo marmore (Balle iaces).*

which may be rather freely translated as:

(Ball, you are dead), who for all were a pattern of life full of honour
    Sweet sounding trumpet of words, orator, (Ball, you are dead)
Father to those who were poor, Consolation to those who were sick, and
    Fame for this church through your great (ah!) merits. (Ball, you are dead)
Near to the bones of your dearly loved friend Bishop Bickley you lie here
    Under this stone touching his, here, alas, Ball, you are dead.

Tricks of verse were common, and acrostics are found on a few brasses, such as one at Northleach, Gloucestershire. Anagrams appear on a few more, one turning the name Hester Manfield of Taplow, Buckinghamshire, into 'Mars fled in thee' with a verse to explain it; she is also described as having died 'in the Catholique Romane faith' in 1617. A hint of religious differences is seen in another inscription in the same church, dated 1564:

Within thys grave ys worthy Ursula layd
Whos honest lyff uppon great vertues stay'd.
The worde of God she held her days so dere
And to her deathe therin she shone so clere
That neither payn ne yett the pryson straynge
Could move her mynd or make her hart to chaynge.
When blessyd lyff had Rydde her from that yll
With syckenes sharpe she was termentyd styll.
Thus free from bandys she fell in bandys ageyn,
As all thyng here ys borne to wo and payn.
O dolefull death thowe art the causer of thys
That Thomas Jonys his worthy wyff doth mys.

Apparently she was imprisoned during the religious persecutions. Another inscription to a convict occurs at Lindfield, Sussex, to Isaac Allen, 1656: 'Hee dyed at London, a Prisoner to ye Upper Bench, vpon an accon for Wordes, most Falsely & Maliciously, by One single Witness sworne against Him, as he had oftentymes, & on his Death-bed Protested & Declared to severall Friends. Hee desired his Body might bee buryed heere at Lindfield (sic) neare his Mother'. The Upper Bench was the Cromwellian equivalent of the King's Bench. Another Sussex man who got into trouble with the Commonwealth was William Cox of Tillington near Petworth, 'an outspoken defender of the orthodox faith, who suffered unjustly at the hands of the rebels for his stalwart loyalty to his King, and who entered the arena in the parish church of Petworth in this county against Fisher, the Antipaedobaptist prize-fighter, and after a fight worth remembering emerged as a strong athelete and a glorious victor'.

An earlier champion of orthodoxy was Bishop Stanbury of Hereford who 'put the wolf to flight from his flock', referring to his suppression of the Lollards.

Unusual professions are found in inscriptions, as are innumerable offices at court, particularly during the Tudor dynasty. Robert Rochester from St Helen's Bishopsgate, London, is described as 'sergeant of the pantry of our sovarn Lord king Henry the VIII', and Alice Baldwin of Lullingstone, Kent, was 'late gentilwoman to the ladi mary princes of England'. When titles and names of professions are translated into Latin there is often some confusion and many prefer to leave the English word in a Latin sentence, as at St Mary-le-Wigford, Lincoln: *'Hic jacet Johannes Jobsun Fychmonger olim vicicomes civitatis Lincoline'*—'Here lies John Jobson, Fishmonger and once Sheriff of the city of Lincoln'. At Bodiam, Sussex, there is an inscription to William Wetherden 'who, while he was uneducated, married, but after his wife's death studied the liberal arts and took holy orders'. A similar inscription at Winwick, Lancashire, is illustrated with the figures of a man wearing a chasuble over his armour, standing beside his wife. Another brass to a priest, at Faversham, Kent, records that he lived for eight years as an anchorite in the church; and a 'heremita' or hermit is commemorated at Wellingham near Fakenham, Norfolk.

Many inscriptions do not show the resignation towards death of the Aldeburgh and Graffham inscriptions already quoted, but complain bitterly. An example from Wormington, Gloucestershire, to a mother, dated 1605 (Fig 16) says:

> *Filiolus, coniux, pater effera fata queruntur*
> *Quae dilectam Annam Savage eripuere marito*
> *Et primogenitam Daston: velut altera phaenix*
> *Dum parit illa perit, dum parturit interit Anna*
> *Anna anima e coelo, lustris iam quinque peractis*
> *In coelam redijt, sed terrae huic ossa reliquit.*

Husband and father and son complain of the fierceness of fate
Fate which has snatched Anne Savage away from the love of her mate,
And too her eldest child Daston: for she like a Phoenix returned
Bringing to birth came to death; Anne, while giving life, death discerned.
Five times five had the years rolled by when Anne, who from God
Gained her soul now gave it back but left her bones under this sod.

A more fanciful attitude is shown in the inscription to Meneleb Rainsford, aged 9, at Henfield, Sussex (Fig 60):

> Great Jove hath lost his Ganymede I know
> Which made him seek an other here below
> And findinge none, not one like unto this,
> Hath ta'en him hence into eternall bliss.
> Cease then for thy deer Meneleb to weep,
> God's darlinge was too good for thee to keep,

> But rather joye in this great favour given:
> A child on earth is made a Saint in Heaven.

An equally pagan and fanciful inscription in St Anne's church, Lewes, Sussex, imagines Hippocrates gazing down and, seeing the great Dr Twyne dead, prophesying terrible plagues for Sussex bereaved of his medical skill.

One of the most moving and philosophical sentiments in an epitaph appears in this inscription from St John's College, Oxford:

*In hac cistula conduntur Exuviae Guilielmi Laud, Archiepiscopi Cantuariensis, qui securi percussus immortalitatem adiit, die decimo Ianuarii An° Dn̄i 1644 Aetatis autem suae 72, Archiepiscopi 11.*

> *Qui fui in Extremis, fortunam expertus utramque*
> *Nemo magis foelix, et mage nemo miser.*
> *Iam Portum inveni: fluitantia secla valete,*
> *Ludite nunc alios, Pax erit alta mihi.*

*Memoriae dn̄i sui in aeternum honorandi posuit Guil. Dell, servus moestissimus.*

In this urn are contained the remains of William Laud, Archbishop of Canterbury, who, at the blow of an axe, attained immortality on the 10th of January, 1644, aged 72, in the 11th year of his archbishopric.

> I, in a life of extremes, saw both sides of Fortune's wheel:
> No one more happy that I, no one more wretched to die.
> Now I have found a harbour, so, storm tossed century, farewell:
> Play now with others, for I now shall have rest on high.

William Dell, his sorrowful servant, placed this to honour his master's memory for ever.

Consolation through trust in God is the theme of many inscriptions, particularly before the Reformation. This mid fifteenth-century verse from Buxted, Sussex, is quite cheerful in its reliance on God's mercy:

> Here lyth graven under this stoon
> Christine Savage, bothe flessh and boon
> Robert huyre sone was persone [parson] heere
> Moore than xxiiij yeere
> Crist godys sone borne of a mayde
> To Christine and Robert huyre sone forsaide
> That out of this world ben passed us fro
> Graunte thy mercy and to us also. Amen.

Nearly all pre-Reformation inscriptions are coupled with a prayer for the soul of the dead man, either direct to God, or beseeching the passer-by to pray on the dead man's behalf. An early French inscription from Woodchurch, Kent, runs as follows:

> *Mestre Nichol de Gore gist en ceste place,*
> *Ihesu Crist prioms ore qe merci lui face.*

In this place lies Master Nichol de Gore,
That he may have mercy, Jesus Christ we adore.

Many inscriptions offer an indulgence for prayers, that is the remission of the temporal punishment due for sin equal to that which would be gained by so many days' fasting and penance. Others, echoing the Lord's Prayer, urge that 'as ye wold be prayed for, pray for us'.

Many figures on brasses are shown with scrolls issuing from their mouths bearing prayers, usually phrases from the Psalms or other scriptures; long passages are divided up among several scrolls. A favourite quotation is Job, xix, 25–7, which appears on marginal inscriptions, on scrolls or on the orphreys of vestments, and runs: *'Credo quod Redemptor meus vivit, et in novissimo die de terra surrecturus sum, et rursum circumdabor pelle mea et in carne mea videbo Deum salvatorem meum; haec spes reposita est in sinu meo'*. It is often paraphrased, and occasionally translated, as at West Hanney, near Wantage, Berkshire: 'I am suer that my Redemer lyveth and that I shall ryse out of the Earthe in the laste Daye and I shallbe covered agayne wythe my skyne and se God in my flesshe, whome I my selfe shall beholde not withe other but withe these same eyes, this hope is puttup in my Bosome.'

Other inscriptions often repeated are verses addressed to the reader, such as *'Quisquis eris'* quoted on p 16, and *'vermibus'*, as follows:

*Vermibus ut donor sic hic ostendere conor*
*Et sicut hic ponor ponitur omnis honor.*
*Hinc tu qui transis magnus medius puer an sis*
*Pro me funde preces ut sit mihi veniae spes.*

Here I am given to worms as here I attempt to show,
And down this path to the grave every honour must go.
You who pass by the way, whether aged or upright or boy,
Pour out prayers for me that I may have hope of joy.

Some prayers are addressed directly to God, and others to saints, whose images are depicted, begging them to intercede with God. Most common are prayers to the Virgin Mary, such as:

*O virgo virginum, ora pro nobis tuum filium.*
O Virgin of Virgins, pray to your Son for us.

Other saints are addressed by name, as in this hexameter line to St Amphibalus:

*Me precor Amphibale salvans ad sidera sume.*
Amphibalus, I pray, save me and lift me on high.

After the Reformation prayers almost come to an end, the few brasses that have scrolls usually venturing no more than 'O praise the Lord'.

At Christ Church, Oxford, and the Temple, London, there are inscriptions composed of several scrolls, that at the Temple church being most elaborate, with twenty-nine heraldic shields. Genealogical inscriptions are found on a few brasses, such as that to Mary Howard of Firle, Sussex (Fig 69), who was married to 'Sir William Howard eldest sonne to S$^r$ Philip Howard sonne and heire to y$^e$ Lord William Howard youngest sonne to y$^e$ Duke of Norfolk'. Some brasses not only give the genealogy but also illustrate it with a series of figures.

Many brasses record at great length the generosity of the deceased, usually legacies given to or through the parish. Thus seven Essex churches have brasses recording the legacies to each by Ralph Rampston, 1585, and six Hampshire churches record the generosity of Thomas Sympson, 1674. One of the most unusual positions for a brass is a pillar on the road between Penrith and Appleby, Cumberland, recording the benefaction of the Countess of Pembroke in 1636, by which charity was to be distributed to the poor from a stone table next to the pillar.

There is a curious record of a benefaction and its fate at Brightling near Battle, Sussex. An inscription dated 1476, which formerly had a figure, records that John Batys gave the floor and seats for the church, and a piece of land called 'Levettys' for the use of the parish. Below is another inscription, which records at great length how 'the good intention of the said Master John Batys was by some ill-mynde deverted, and the lands called Levytts converted to private use from this Church for many yeres, and the said inscription devised by the said Master Batys to this tombe stone was then by unjust hands broken and purloyned' and that over 150 years later, after a long suit in Chancery, the land was restored to the church and the new inscription put up to record it in 1635 'Ratyfyed and confirmed in all poynts'. The old inscription it seems was found at the bottom of a well on the Downs.

A few inscriptions include puns on the name of the deceased, such as one in the same church of Brightling to Thomas Pye with the motto '*Vive pius, moriere pius*'—'Live pious and die pious'. A more complicated inscription appears in St Michael's, Oxford (Fig 15), where the name John, meaning 'Grace' in Hebrew, is punned with *Gratia* in Latin.

Many inscriptions give two dates or the date 'according to the style used in England', because of the discrepancy between the Julian calendar used in England up to 1752, and the Gregorian calendar adopted by most of the rest of Europe in 1582. By the old calendar the year began on 25 March, so January, February and most of March were reckoned with the year before. The day of the month also varied, since the reformed calendar does not keep a leap year on the first day of a century unless that century is divisible by 400; so by the seventeenth century the English reckoning was

*Page 151* Figure of Lionel, Duke of Clarence, from tomb of
Edward III, 1377, Westminster Abbey

*Page 152* Tomb of William Longspee, 1226, Salisbury Cathedral

ten days ahead of the Continental, and eleven days ahead by 1752 when the reform was adopted in England. Inscriptions may give two dates as if they were a fraction, viz $\frac{10}{20}$ January 164$\frac{3}{4}$. None of these discrepancies of date, however, can explain the inscription at Adderbury, Oxfordshire, dated 30 February.

Many sentimental epitaphs were composed by the bereaved husband or wife, though a few fine compositions are found, such as this verse in the metaphysical style, from Mulbarton near Norwich, 1680.

> Dear love, one Feather'd minute & I come
> To lye down in thy darke Retireing Roome
> And mingle dust with Thine: yt wee may have
> As when alive one bed, so dead one grave.
> And may my Soul teare through the vaulted sky
> To be with thine to all Eternity.
> O How our Bloudless formes will y$^t$ day greet
> With Love Divine when we again shall meet
> Devest of all Contagion of the Flesh
> Fullfill'd with everlasting joys & Fresh
> In Heaven above, And ('t may be) cast an eye
> How far Elizium doth beneath us lye.
> Deare, I disbody and away
> More Swift than Wind
> Or Flying Hind,
> I come, I come away.

K

# 7 ❦ The Copying and Study of Brasses

IT IS A peculiarity of brasses that they can be studied as well, if not better, in reproduction than in the original. It is comparatively easy to make exact reproductions, and much easier to study them than to examine brasses in their churches. Most of the various methods of reproduction that follow are suitable for incised slabs as well as brasses.

To begin with some problems: many of the best brasses are situated in remote country churches that are difficult to find or get to; some country churches are kept locked and the visitor has to spend time getting the key; and you may find a service, a wedding or a funeral in progress when you get there. Sunday mornings should always be avoided; weddings usually take place on Saturdays, but funerals occur at unpredictable times during the week and the visitor may have to wait a long time for the church to be free.

Once inside the church there are more difficulties. Many small churches, particularly if they have stained glass windows, are very dark, and brasses are often hidden in the darkest corners, overshadowed by pews or pillars. Occasionally the visitor may be able to do no more than feel the brass without being able to see it at all. Even if the church is well lit the brass may be black with age and the design quite invisible. Some brasses are even further hidden by carpets, pews or even a raised floor. At Battle, Sussex, one brass can only be seen by taking up some loose floorboards, while at Dyrham near Bristol the brass is only exposed in the summer months when the whole floor is taken up. Some brasses, such as the huge Nelond brass at Cowfold, Sussex, are kept under locked covers and can only be viewed by appointment. Finally the visitor may be forestalled by brass-rubbers who completely obscure the monument they are working on.

In the face of all these difficulties many people will be glad to sacrifice the sight of the brass in its setting in favour of an easily accessible reproduction. There are good collections of reproductions in London, the chief being the British Museum collection, including the prints made in the late eighteenth century by Craven Ord, which show many brasses since lost or mutilated. There are also the Victoria and Albert Museum collection, of which an illustrated catalogue is published; the Society of Antiquaries collection, which is the largest and also contains rubbings of many lost brasses; and good collections at the Bodleian Library and Ashmolean Museum in Oxford, and the Cambridge Museum of Archaeology and Ethnology.

While these are excellent collections, not everyone can have access to them, and so the most satisfactory and rewarding alternative is to make one's own collection. One is then able to see the brass in its setting and have a reproduction of it ready to hand, and the collection has the advantage of being based on one's own choice of subject.

There are many methods of reproducing brasses or incised slabs, but the commonest is by *rubbing*. The basic technique of brass-rubbing was introduced to most of us with a penny and a pencil. It is almost certainly the method of copying an inscription referred to in the last scene of *Timon of Athens*:

> My noble general, Timon is dead;
> Entomb'd upon the very hem o' the sea;
> And on his grave-stone this insculpture, which
> With wax I brought away, whose soft impression
> Interprets for my poor ignorance.

A few brass-rubbings survive from the eighteenth century, but they did not become popular until the nineteenth. Since then their popularity has fluctuated, reaching a peak in recent years both among students with some real interest in brasses and others who only desire 'artistic creation' without art or effort.

The first step towards making a brass-rubbing is to get permission from the relevant authority, which is usually the rector or vicar in a parish church or the dean in a cathedral, though sometimes authority is delegated to a verger or churchwarden. A few incumbents leave a notice in the church to say that no permission is needed, but these are rare; sometimes the rubber must write for permission two or three months in advance, as a popular brass may be reserved for weeks ahead. When writing for permission it is best to enclose a stamped addressed envelope and also to suggest alternative dates for the visit. If the brass is in a remote church, however, and is not well known, it is usually possible to get permission on the day the rubbing is to be made.

The attitudes of the clergy towards brass-rubbers vary tremendously: some will refuse any payment and may even invite the rubber to tea, others charge a small fee but willingly reduce it for students, and others charge a high fee, in one case as high as £25. Some clergy also insist on a rubber signing a legal undertaking not to sell the rubbings, and assigning a church-warden to supervise the work. An increasing number of churches now refuse permission altogether, for a variety of reasons. The most usual are that the brasses are worn or that the rubbers have damaged them. Rubbing does not in fact normally wear the brass at all and if one rubber has damaged a brass it is false logic, if human nature, to assume that all brass-rubbers damage brasses. Many incumbents complain of the conduct of rubbers, who have brought transistors into the church, allowed children to play in the sanctuary or left picnic litter behind them. It is, of course, a matter of common decency not to abuse the incumbent's trust in such a way and to be careful not to tread on rolled-up carpets, upset flower vases or leave the church untidy. Another frequent complaint is that rubbings are sold at high prices and the church exploited, sometimes without even the permission of the incumbent. Some incumbents shelter behind their parish councils, saying that they would be delighted to give permission but the council will not allow it, though legally the incumbent himself has absolute control over the brasses.

Once the rubber has secured permission he must collect the materials necessary. The first is *heelball*, which is a cake or stick of black wax, originally invented for blackening shoe-leather. It can be bought in most shops dealing in artists' materials, but the best heelball, made for the Monumental Brass Society, can only be bought from Phillips and Page Ltd, 50 Church Street, Kensington, London. This is the hardest and will give a shiny black surface when polished.

Paper is also needed and there is a wider choice here, provided only that it be strong enough to resist the pressure of the heelball and thin enough to give a clear impression. The paper usually recommended is architect's detail paper, but this is expensive and has a shiny surface on which it is difficult to make a good rubbing. Ordinary lining paper is cheap and easy to use and can be bought from any shop dealing in wallpapers; it comes in rolls 22 in (56 cm) wide, and brasses wider than that can be done in strips. This narrow paper is far easier to handle and transport than wider paper; it also matures to a cream colour, which provides a more pleasing contrast with the black of the heelball than a dead white paper.

The other requirements are dusters to clean the brass and polish the rubbing and tape to hold the paper in place. Masking tape is the best for this job, as it sticks to stone better than cellulose tape and with care does not damage painted walls adjacent to the brass. Cellulose tape is liable to mark the wall permanently and is rightly forbidden by some incumbents. No tape, however, will stick on flaky stone such as chalk or sandstone.

Once in a church, as we have seen, the brass must be found. If it is high up, one will usually be able to borrow a ladder from the vestry, and occasionally the clergy will even volunteer to hold the ladder during rubbing. Some brasses, however, need acrobatics to reach them: I have done rubbings while standing with one foot on the edge of a pew-back, steadying myself with one hand and holding the paper with my head. If necessary, permission must be asked to turn on the church lights to illuminate brasses in dark corners.

The brass must be carefully brushed before work begins, specially if it has been under a carpet or is set in flaky stone, since dust and grit will spoil the rubbing and sometimes even scratch the brass. The paper should then be unrolled over the brass and, if possible, taped in position. If this is not possible, help is needed to hold the paper on mural brasses, but if the brass is on the floor the paper can be held by weights or knelt on, taking care not to scratch the brass with shoes. If the brass is too wide for the paper it must, as I have said, be done in strips allowing plenty of overlap.

The reproduction of the brass can now be made by rubbing the heelball over the paper on top of the brass. This produces a clear reproduction on which the metal surfaces appear black and the engraved lines are left white. To get a good black surface quite hard work may be necessary and a large brass can take several hours to rub.

The whole brass should be rubbed and, indeed, it is wise to rub over the stone all round the brass in case projecting parts such as swords or spurs are left out. Many rubbers make a point of never going 'over the edge' of the plates, but this usually leads to omissions. If any of the brass is missing the indents should be outlined and any rivets surviving in these indents also rubbed. If there is a lot lost it is sometimes better to rub the entire slab (as in Figs 9 and 28). The rubber, however, should never let the heelball go off the edge of the paper as it leaves a permanent mark. Great care should be taken to avoid tearing the paper by letting the heelball fall into indents or hit projecting rivets. While all rivets were originally flush with the surface of the brass, many have worked out or been replaced with round-headed screws, and such obstacles should be noted before beginning the rubbing. As well as complete rubbings, duplicates can be made of attractive details. The finished rubbing can be polished with a duster before taking up the paper. When clearing up afterwards it is a good idea to collect up any chips of heelball that may be lying on the paper, as these can be saved and melted down to make a new cake. They should not be scattered over the church floor, as many rubbers do.

This is the most usual way of rubbing a brass but there are others. The brass-rubber can use white heelball and then darken the lines with Indian ink to give black lines and a white surface; but this is difficult and the effect usually messy and unsatisfactory. Rubbings can also be done with different coloured heelballs on coloured paper but these, while perhaps more decorative, are not so clear, nor so valuable as reproductions.

A useful method of rubbing for reproducing worn or lightly engraved brasses is *dabbing*. The equipment consists of a pad or ball of leather and a tin of black paste made of powdered graphite and olive oil. The pad is dipped in the paste and worked up and down on a sheet of cardboard to spread the paste evenly, and the rubbing is then done with the blackened leather pad. The great advantage of this method is that little or no friction is produced and so one can use very thin paper, even tissue-paper, which will copy details too fine to show up on the thicker paper needed for heelball rubbing. The reproduction is grey not black. Very much the same technique can be used with lino printing ink and a rubber roller, which works particularly well on incised slabs, indents or lightly engraved brasses, and can produce as black a surface as heelball though without the shine. Experience, however, is needed before an even covering is achieved.

Before leaving the church, check any interesting facts about the brass or its subject in the church guide, note down the colour of any shields that can be seen, and sketch any carved monument or frame to the brass.

Once home, assemble any rubbings that have been done in strips. They should be laid out on the floor, the margin of the overlap cut off, and pasted together with the greatest care that all parts be correctly positioned. The best paste to use is ordinary flour paste made by boiling together flour and water. This can be used either hot or cold and has the great advantage that it does not stick immediately, so the sheets of paper can be adjusted to the right position after the paste has been spread on.

Most brass-rubbers will want to hang some of their rubbings, and it is best they be mounted first, which not only improves their appearance but also strengthens them. Many serious collectors condemn all mounting, as most people when mounting leave out indents of missing parts and even some of the brass itself, thus ruining it as a historical record. However, there is no reason why a rubbing should not be as valuable mounted as not.

Before cutting out the rubbing it should be laid over the backing paper, which can be of any kind, and a number of points pricked through to serve as a key to reassembling the rubbing. The various parts of the rubbing are then cut out and pasted into the positions marked. Any indents should be traced on and the positions of surviving rivets marked on them. The ends of the paper should then be reinforced with strips of wood or bamboo from which the rubbings can be hung.

Rubbings can be treated in a variety of ways to make them more attractive. As long as the collector can be sure of what has been lost, missing parts can be restored (as in Fig 45), though a note should always be made of what parts are so treated. The restoration can be carried out either by drawing in the design with Indian ink or by pasting on duplicate rubbings of corresponding parts of the brass. Any parts that have been or still are coloured can be painted on the rubbing with lacquer paints. On shields, tabards and other heraldic devices, the proper colours must always be used, but there is scope for a little imagination in other directions. Armour can be painted silver and the whole rubbing gilded to reproduce the appearance of the original. The painter should not, however, attempt realistic colouring, as this is out of key with the medium of line drawing, and the contrast of surface and line must be preserved in any accurate rendering.

To clarify a rubbing, or to hide any blemishes on the surface, black and white Indian ink may be applied with a paintbrush. It will normally cover heelball without difficulty, but if the grease in the heelball resists it, treat the rubbing with a little methylated spirit to dissolve the grease. The collector should be moderate in the use of ink because it is almost impossible to keep exactly to the lines, specially if a brass has a lot of fine shading.

To 'reverse' a rubbing, to give black lines on a white surface, the collector can fill in the lines with Indian ink and then scrub off the heelball with a paraffin-soaked rag. The lines, however, usually blur and, like the alternative method of reversal described on p 158, the effect is not really satisfactory.

All these methods of making a rubbing more decorative detract from its clarity and value as a historical record. If a serious collection is planned, therefore, it is better to make a spare copy of any brass required for decoration and keep the master copy in its natural state for reference. While using rubbings as decorations, the collector should never lose sight of their real value, nor of the purpose for which their originals were made, and should treat them with the dignity due to the monuments of the dead. While rubbings may be hung with some dignity on the walls of a room, to stick them on wastepaper-baskets or on the sides of baths, as has been done too often, is to demean oneself and make a mockery of their message: 'Look: such as we are, such shall you be'.

A large collection of rubbings is difficult to store. Rolled rubbings tend to tear badly and are also difficult to examine, as after some time they will not flatten out; and folded rubbings are easier to examine but are liable to tear along the folds, and their appearance is also spoilt, which is a great disadvantage if photographs are wanted. The best method is to keep all rubbings flat, either hanging against a wall or, if they are small, lying in a drawer. Once a collection has grown to any considerable size, however, this method becomes impossible. Rubbings can be kept hanging in racks, but racks are difficult to construct and also take up a lot of space. Part of the Craven Ord collection in the British Museum was originally arranged in a great book, 6 ft high, but this, though interesting, is not really practical as a method of storage. Most collectors will have to keep their rubbings rolled up or folded and repair the tears from time to time. If the rubbings are mounted on linen they will be stronger, but most people would find this too expensive.

For easy access, photographs are more convenient than the rubbings themselves, but these are difficult to take as the shiny black surface reflects light and the slightest irregularity on the surface will show up on the photograph. To get successful photographs the rubbings must be laid absolutely flat and out of all direct light, which is exceptionally difficult to do.

For whatever purpose a rubbing is wanted, it should always be labelled with at least the name of the church and the name and date of the subject as far as these are known. If a serious collection is planned the rubbings should also be catalogued. In addition to the above information, one must give the position of the brass in the church, the date the rubbing was made, a description of the brass, details of any heraldry on it, a clear copy of any inscription surviving, with a translation if necessary, any interesting historical details, and the sizes of the various parts of the brass. It is also useful to give an acquisition number to each rubbing and the number of the brass in Mill Stephenson's *List*, as this is the usual way of referring to it.

Each rubbing should be described on a separate page and these kept in a loose-leaf folder so that they can be rearranged or added to. There are many different ways of arranging a collection, but probably the most usual is to follow Mill Stephenson's *List*: in this the counties are listed alphabetically and the churches alphabetically within each county, the dedication of the church being given only if there is more than one church in the town; and within each church the brasses are arranged chronologically. Other systems of arrangement depend on the interests of the collector: the brasses can be all arranged chronologically; or classified into military, heraldic, monastic or other categories. A more interesting method is to group them stylistically, following the different artistic traditions. These systems are most useful if they are combined with card indexes. A main catalogue should be made, preferably in Mill Stephenson's order, and then a series of card indexes to which cross-references are made using the acquisition number. To give an example, Sir Robert de Bures (Fig 8) would be catalogued under Suffolk, Acton, Number I, with an acquisition number of 254. It would then be indexed under the early fourteenth century as c 1310, its probable date, with possibly a second card as it has for many years been dated at 1302. Also it would be indexed under 'military brasses', 'heraldic brasses', 'Gothic brasses', and grouped with Sir John Daubernoun and Sir Roger de Trumpington and perhaps even 'Brasses with animals'.

Nearly all collections are made with rubbings, as has been described. There are, however, other methods of copying brasses, most of them more curious than practical. The most obvious is to photograph the brass, but in most cases this is impracticable. The original brass never has the clear contrast of black and white that appears on a rubbing, as the lines are usually only a slightly different shade of the surface colour. Unless the brass be very clean and the lines blackened, a photograph will not be clear enough to be of any value. There is also the great problem of lighting the dark corners where brasses are often found, which adds to the expense of photography. The main problem, however, is getting a straight view of the brass: unless it be very small, or mural, it is almost impossible to position the camera directly over the centre of the brass at a long enough range to include the whole composition. The photograph must be taken from the side, and so, of course, the design is distorted by the angle. Photography, therefore, has limited use in recording brasses; and its greatest value is on the stonework surrounding them, such as canopies, frames or altar-tombs, or to record any colouring that may remain on the brass.

Perhaps the most famous of the other methods of reproducing brasses is that used by Craven Ord and Sir John Cullum to make the copies of brasses now in the British Museum. They copied over 200 brasses, mostly from East Anglia, in the late eighteenth century, by the original method described in this letter of 1780, quoted by Haines in his *Manual of Monumental Brasses*:

I spent Saturday morning with Mr Ord to look over his impressions from brasses, which are curiously done; and he has a large collection. The manner in which he does them is this: he has French paper damped, and kept in a tin case made on purpose to keep it so, printer's ink in a bottle, and a quantity of rags; he inks the brass, and then wipes it very clean, lays on the paper, covers it with a cloth, and treads upon it, and takes the impression; and he has a man at home to finish them up with printer's ink where the lines have failed; he then cuts out the figures, and pastes them into a large portfolio, with blue paper leaves, large enough to contain a figure six feet high; and you cannot imagine how beautiful they appear.

The chief value of the Craven Ord collection is its antiquity, as his method has several disadvantages, the greatest being the inevitable reversal of the brasses making the inscriptions quite illegible without a mirror. Nor, I imagine, would this method, which involves pouring ink all over the brasses, be allowed today.

Solid copies of brasses can also of course be made by electrotype. Many re-used brasses have been copied in this way, so that both sides of the plate can be available for rubbing without keeping the brass loose. It also is very expensive. A cheaper method used in some churches for the same purpose is to make lino cuts, but these need great skill and accuracy. Plastic moulds have also been made of the reverses of brasses, a very accurate but still expensive method.

Finally it is always possible to make freehand drawings of brasses. All early books on the subject are illustrated with such drawings, which may range from painfully crude sketches to the very fine drawings engraved by Wenceslaus Hollar of the brasses formerly in Old St Paul's Cathedral. But such drawings call for great artistic skill and do not fall into the same category as the methods of reproducing brasses described above.

There is, therefore, a wide choice of methods for reproducing brasses and arranging a collection of such reproductions. The study of brasses is far too wide a subject to be covered in any one book, and others are suggested in the bibliography. But one can never appreciate such a subject by reading alone. Some idea of its depth and variety can be gained by glancing through any issue of the Monumental Brass Society's *Transactions*. Anyone who is interested in brasses can join this society, whose aims are the study and preservation of brasses, incised slabs and indents, not only in England but all over the world. For information on the subject or concerning admission to the society, one should write to the Secretary, c/o the Society of Antiquaries, Burlington House, London W1. Most counties have archaeological societies whose activities include the study of brasses, and their publications often contain very useful descriptions of local brasses. The addresses of these societies can be found in the relevant county libraries.

# SELECT BIBLIOGRAPHY

Ashmolean Museum, Oxford. *Notes on Brass-Rubbing* (1941, revised 1969)
Bouquet, Dr A. C. *Church Brasses* (1956)
Boutell, Rev C. *Monumental Brasses and Slabs* (1847); *The Monumental Brasses of England, a Series of Engravings on Wood* (1849)
Busby, R. *Beginners' Guide to Brass Rubbing* (1969)
Franklyn, J. *Brasses* (1964)
Gittings, C. *Brasses and Brass Rubbings* (1970)
Gough, R. *Sepulchral Monuments of Great Britain* (1786)
Greenhill, F. A. *The Incised Slabs of Leicestershire and Rutland* (1958)
Haines, Rev H. *Manual of Monumental Brasses* (1861)
Macklin, Rev H. W. *Monumental Brasses* (1890, revised 1913); *The Brasses of England* (1907)
Mann, Sir J. *Monumental Brasses* (1957)
Monumental Brass Society. *Transactions and Portfolio 1887–1914*, 1934+
Norris, M. *Brass Rubbing* (1965)
Page-Phillips, J. C. *Macklin's Monumental Brasses* (1969)
Stephenson, Mill. *A List of Monumental Brasses in the British Isles* (1926) with *Appendix* (1936) (reprinted with Appendix 1964)
Victoria and Albert Museum. *Catalogue of Brass-Rubbings* (1929, reprinted 1968)
Weever, J. *Ancient Funeral Monuments* (1631)

# LIST OF BRASSES AND INDEX

The following list includes all recorded figure brasses but inscriptions only when they are referred to in the text. For a complete list of all brasses see *A List of Monumental Brasses in the British Isles* by Mill Stephenson. In all cases the reference is to the main parish church unless otherwise specified.

References to the text are given in brackets after the dates and illustration numbers in italics.

*Abbreviations*

| | | | |
|---|---|---|---|
| Ac: | academic gowns | L: | lady |
| br: | bracket | M: | military |
| C: | civilian or lay figure | pal: | palimpsest |
| ca: | canopy | S: | shroud |
| E: | ecclesiastic | SS: | saints |
| her: | heraldic | sym: | symbolic or allegorical |
| ins: | inscription | * | large or especially interesting |
| IS: | incised slab | + | cross |

Brackets round an abbreviation indicate that the figure or design is badly mutilated. Entries such as C, L, 1450, 1506 mean that there are brasses both to a civilian and a lady on both those dates. Entries such as C, 1415, 1415 mean that there are two separate civilian brasses for that date.

L

Wilbraham, Little, Cambridge: Ac, 1521.
Wilburton, Ely: E, ca, * 1477; C, L, 1506, 1516 (59).
Wimpole, Royston: E, SS, 1501; C, c 1500; L, c 1535.
Wisbech: M, * 1401.
Wood Ditton, Newmarket: M, (L), * 1393.

CHESHIRE

Chester, St Peter: C, c 1460.
Macclesfield: C, L, sym, 1506 (131).
Malpas: 24 ins, (52).
Middlewich: L, 1591.
Over, Winsford: M, c 1510.
Wilmslow: M, L, ca, * 1460.
Wybunbury, Nantwich: M, L, 1513.

CORNWALL

Antony, East, Millbrook: L, ca, * 1420.
Blisland, Bodmin: E, 1410.
Budock, Falmouth: M, L, 1567.
Callington: Judge, L, 1465.
Cardinham, Bodmin: E, c 1400.
Colan, Newquay: C, L, 1572; M, L, 1575.
Constantine, Helston: C, L, pal, 1574; C, L, 1616.
Crowan, Camborne: M, c 1420; M, L, c 1490; (M, L), c 1550; (M), 1599, fragments.
Fowey: C, L, c 1450; C, c 1450; C, 1582; L, 1602.
Goran, St Austell: L, c 1510.
Grade, Lizard: M, L, 1522.
Helston: C, L, 1606.
Illogan, Redruth: M, L, 1603.
Landrake, Saltash: M, 1509.
Lanteglos, Fowey: M, * c 1440; M, L, c 1525.
Launceston: L, c 1620.
Lostwithiel: M, 1423.
Madron, Penzance: C, L, 1623.
Mawgan-in-Pyder, Newquay: E, c 1420; M, L, 1573; L, 1578; C, c 1580; fragments
    (137).
Probus, Truro: C, L, 1514.
Quethioc, Callington: C, L, 1471, 1631.
St Breock, Wadebridge: C, L, c 1510.
St Columb Major, Newquay: M, L, L, 1545; M, L, 1633, 1633.
St Erme, Truro: C, L, 1596.
St Gluvias, Falmouth: C, L, c 1485.
St Ives: L, SS, 1462.
St Just, Truro: E, c 1520.
St Mellion, Callington: M, L, * 1551.
St Michael Penkivil, Truro: M, 1497; Ac, 1515; C, L, 1619; L, 1622; M, 1634.
St Minver, Wadebridge: C, 1517.
Sithney, Helston: +, c 1420.
Stratton, Bude: M, L, L, 1561.
Tintagel: L, c 1430.

Truro Cathedral: C, L, 1585; C, 1630.
Wendron, Helston: (E), 1535; C, L, c 1580.


### CUMBERLAND

Bootle, Millom: M, 1562.
Caslisle Cathedral: Bishop, * 1496, * 1616 (75) cf Oxford, The Queen's College.
Crosthwaite, Keswick: M, L, 1527.
Edenhall, Penrith: M, L, her, * 1458.
Greystoke, Penrith: E, 1526; L, c 1540, 1547; C, 1551.
Penrith (by roadside): ins, 1636 (150).
Westward, Wigton: sym, 1648.


### DERBYSHIRE

Ashbourne: ins, 1241?; M, L, her, ca, * 1538.
Ashover, Matlock: E, 1504; M, L, 1507.
Bakewell: C, 1648.
Beeley, Bakewell: S, 1710.
Chesterfield: (L), 1451; M, L, her, 1529.
Crich, Alfreton: Child, 1637.
Dronfield: E, E, 1399; C, L, 1580; 14 ins.
Edensor, Bakewell: M, 1570.
Etwall, Derby: L, SS, 1512; M, L, L, her, 1557.
Hathersage: M, L, 1463, 1493; M, L, her, 1500, c 1560.
Hope, Hathersage: C, 1685.
Kedleston, Derby: M, L, 1496.
Longstone, Great, Bakewell: C, L, sym, 1624.
Morley, Derby: M, L, SS, 1454; M, L, L, SS, 1470; M, 3L, * 1481; M, L, SS,
    c 1525; M, L, 1558.
Mugginton, Derby: M, L, * c 1475.
Norbury, Ashbourne: Judge, L, pal, * 1558.
Sawley, Long Eaton: M, L, 1467, 1478; C, L, 1510.
Staveley: M, her, sym, c 1480; M, L, SS, 1503.
Taddington, Buxton: C, L, 1505.
Tideswell, Buxton: sym, 1462; C, L, c 1500; Bishop, 1579 (96).
Walton-on-Trent, Burton: E, 1492.
Wilne, Long Eaton: M, M, L, her, sym, 1513.
Wirksworth: C, L, c 1510, 1525.


### DEVONSHIRE

Allington, East, Dartmouth: L, c 1450; C, L, 1595.
Atherington, Barnstaple: M, L, L, 1539.
Bigbury, Kingsbridge: L, c 1440, c 1460.
Blackawton, Dartmouth: C, L, 1582.
Braunton, Barnstaple: L, 1548.
Chittlehampton, Molton: C, L, L, 1480.
Clovelly: M, 1540, c 1540.
Clyst St George, Exeter: L, 1614.
Dartmouth, St Petrock: C, 1609; L, 1610, 1617.
— St Saviour: M, L, L, ca, * 1408; L, c 1470; C, 1637.

Ermington, Modbury: C, L, 1583.
Exeter Cathedral: M, ca, 1409; E, * 1413.
Filleigh, Molton: M, 1570, 1570.
Haccombe, Newton Abbot: M, 1469, 1586; L, 1589, 1611; M, L, 1656.
Harford, Plympton: M, 1566; C, L, 1639.
Hartland: L, 1610.
Luppitt, Honiton: (L), pal, c 1440/c 1400.
Monkleigh, Bideford: sym, 1509; M, 1566.
Otterton, Sidmouth: Children, 1641, 1641.
Ottery St Mary, Honiton: C, C, C, c 1620.
Petrockstow, Torrington: M, L, 1591.
St Giles-in-the-Wood, Torrington: L, 1430, 1592, 1610.
Sampford Peverell: L, 1602.
Sandford, Crediton: L, 1604.
Shillingford, Bampton: M, L, her, 1499.
Staverton, Totnes: C, 1592.
Stoke Fleming, Dartmouth: C, L, ca, * 1391 (126).
Stoke-in-Teignhead: E, c 1370.
Tedburn St Mary, Crediton: Ac, 1580; E, L, 1613.
Tiverton: C, L, 1529.
Tor Mohun, Torquay: L, 1581.
Ugborough, Modbury: L, c 1500.
Washfield, Tiverton: C, L, 1606.
Yealmpton, Plympton: M, 1508; ins, pal, 1580.

### DORSET

Bere Regis: C, L, 1596.
Church Knowle, Wareham: M, L, L, 1572.
Compton Valence, Dorchester: E, c 1440.
Corfe Mullen, Wimborne Minster: C, 1437.
Crichel More, Cranbourne: L, 1572.
Evershot, Yetminster: E, 1524.
Fleet, Weymouth: M, L, 1603, 1612.
Langton, Blandford: C, L, L, 1467.
Lytchett Matravers, Upton: ins, her, 1364 (122); S, c 1470.
Melbury Sampford, Yetminster: M, her, 1562.
Milton Abbey, Blandford: M, her, 1565.
Moreton, Bere Regis: M, 1523.
Piddlehinton, Piddletown: ins, pal, 1562; E, 1617.
Piddletown: C, 1517; M, her, sym, 1524; M, L, 1595.
Pimperne, Blandford: L, S, 1694 (52, 77, 106, 113, 22).
Puncknowle, Bridport: M, c 1600.
Purse Caundle, Sherborne: M, c 1500; L, 1527; (E), 1536.
Rampisham, Beaminster: C, L, 1523.
Shapwick, Sturminster: L, c 1440; E, c 1520.
Sturminster Marshall: E, 1581.
Swanage: L, L, c 1490.
Thorncombe, Crewkerne: C, L, * 1437.
Wimborne Minster: King, c 1440 (19, 30).
Winterbourne Came, Dorchester: L, 1620.
Woolland, Sturminster: L, 1616.
Yetminster: M, L, * 1531.

DURHAM

Auckland, St Andrew: E, c 1380; +, sym, 1581.
Auckland, St Helen: C, (L), c 1470.
Billingham, Stockton: (E), c 1480.
Brancepeth: M, c 1400; Ac, 1456.
Chester-le-Street, Durham: L, 1430.
Durham Cathedral: Large indent, 1333 (16, 35, 126).
Hartlepool: L, 1593.
Haughton-le-Skerne, Darlington: L, 1592.
Houghton-le-Spring: L, 1587.
Sedgefield: L, * c 1310, stolen in 1969 (66, 98); S, c 1500.


ESSEX (excluding London area)

Althorne, Burnham-on-Crouch: SS, 1502; C, sym, 1508.
Arkesden, Saffron Walden: M, 1439.
Ashen, Yeldham: M, L, c 1440.
Aveley, Grays: M, ca, French, * 1370 (115); Children, c 1520, 1583, 1588.
Baddow, Great, Chelmsford: L, 1614.
Bardfield, Great, Finchingfield: L, 1584.
Belchamp St Paul, Yeldham: M, L, 1587.
Bentley, Little, Colchester: M, L, 1490.
Berden, Stansted Mountfitchet: C, L, L, 1473; C, L, 1607.
Blackmore, Brentwood: C, c 1420.
Bocking, Braintree: M, L, 1420; C, 1613.
Boreham, Chelmsford: L, 1573.
Bowers Gifford, Basildon: M, * 1348 (82, 83, 84).
Bradfield, Harwich: L, 1598.
Bradwell-on-Sea: L, 1526.
Braxted, Little, Witham: M, L, L, 1508.
Brentwood, St Thomas: sym, 1671.
Brightlingsea: C, L, 1496; L, 1505, 1514; C, L, L, 1521; C, L, 1525; L, L, 1536; C, 1578.
Bromley, Great, Colchester: E, ca, 1432.
Canfield, Great, Dunmow, L, c 1530; M, L, 1558, 1588.
Canfield, Little, Dunmow: L, L, 1578, 1593.
Chesterton, Great, Saffron Walden: L, c 1530; Child, 1600.
Chesterford, Little, Saffron Walden: L, 1462.
Chigwell, Woodford: Archbishop, ** 1631 (16, 47, 58, 76, 97, 137, 1).
Chrishall, Saffron Walden: M, L, ca*, c 1380; L, c 1450; C, L, 1480.
Clavering, Newport: C, L, c 1480, 1591, 1593.
Coggeshall, Braintree: L, L, c 1490; C, L, c 1520, 1533; C, 1580.
Colchester, St James: C, 1569; (L), 1584.
— St Peter: Alderman, L, 1530, 1533 (25, 110); C, 1563; C, L, 1572, 1610.
Cold Norton, Maldon: L, c 1520.
Corrington, Braintree: E, c 1340; C, c 1460.
Cressing, Basildon: L, 1610.
Dengie, Burnham-on-Couch: L, c 1520.
Donyland, East, Wivenhoe: C, 1621; L, 1627.
Dovercourt, Harwich: C, c 1430.
Dunmow, Great: L, 1579.
Easter, Little, Dunmow: E, c 1420; M, L, her*, 1483 (89, 122).
Eastwood, Southend: C, 1600.

— Museum: many fragments.
Sandon, Chelmsford: E, L, 1588.
Southminster, Burnham: C, L, c 1560; C, 1634.
Springfield, Chelmsford: M, 1421.
Stanford Rivers, Chipping Ongar: Child, 1492; M, L, 1503, c 1540; L, 1584.
Stebbing, Dunmow: L, c 1390.
Stifford, Grays: E, 1378; S, c 1480; C, L, 1504, 1622; L, 1630.
Stisted, Braintree: L, 1584.
Stock, Billericay: M, 1574.
Stondon Massey, Brentwood: C, L, L, 1570; M, L, pal, 1573.
Stow Maries, Maldon: L, 1602.
Strethall, Saffron Walden: Ac, c 1480.
Sutton, Southend: Sergeant-at-arms, 1371.
Terling, Braintree: M, L, c 1500; C, L, 1584; C, L, L, 1584.
Thaxted: Ac, c 1450.
Theydon Gernon, Epping: E, 1458; M, L, c 1520; L, 1567.
Thorrington, Brightlingsea: L, 1564.
Thurrock, West: C, C, 1585.
Tillingham, Burnham-on-Crouch: C, 1584.
Tilty, Dunmow: M, L, 1520, 1562; L, 1590.
Tollesbury, Maldon: C, L, 1517.
Tolleshunt D'Arcy, Maldon: SS, pal, Flemish, c 1350; M, L, c 1420; L, pal, c 1535;
    M, c 1540; L, 1559.
Toppesfield, Steeple Bumpsted: C, L, 1534.
Totham, Great, Witham: L, 1606.
Twinstead, Sudbury: C, L, 1610.
Waltham Abbey, Cheshunt: C, C, L, 1565; C, L, 1576.
Waltham, Great, Chelmsford: C, L, 1580; C, c 1580; C, L, 1617.
Waltham, Little, Chelmsford: M, 1447.
Warley, Little, Brentwood: L, 1592.
Weald, North, Epping: C, L, 1606.
Weald, South, Brentwood: C, c 1450; L, c 1460; C, c 1480; Judge, L, 1567; C, c 1600;
    fragments.
Wendon Lofts, Saffron Walden: C, L, c 1460.
Wendens Ambo, Saffron Walden: M, c 1410.
Widdington, Saffron Walden: C, c 1450.
Willingale-Doe, Chelmsford: M, 1442; L, 1582, 1613.
Wimbish, Saffron Walden: M, L, +, * 1347 (49, 66, 82, 84, 132).
Wivenhoe, Colchester: M, ca, * 1507; E, 1535; L, ca, her, * 1537.
Woodham Mortimer, Maldon: Child, 1584.
Wormingford, Colchester: C, c 1460; C, L, L, c 1590.
Writtle, Colchester: M, L, c 1500; C, 4L, c 1510; M, L, L, M, 1513; L, 1524;
    C, L, 1576; L, 1592; C, L, 1606, 1616.
Yeldham, Great: C, L, 1612.


## GLOUCESTERSHIRE

Berkeley, Stroud: C, 1526.
Bibury, Cirencester: S, 1707, 1717 (113, *70*).
Bisley, Stroud: L, 1515.
Blockley, Chipping Campden (formerly Worcs): E, 1488, 1510.
Bristol, Grammar School: C, L, L, c 1570 (in upper schoolroom).
— St James: C, L, 1636.
— St John: C, L, 1478.

— St Mary Redcliffe: Judge, L, * 1439; M, L, L, her, sym, 1475; C, L, * c 1480; Sergeant-at-law, L, 1522 (106). Also C, c 1400; E, c 1460; from Temple Church.
— St Stephen: C, L, 1594.
— St Werburgh (new church): C, L, 1586.
— Trinity Almshouse Chapel: C, ca, 1411; L, ca, 1411.
Cheltenham, St Mary: Judge, L, 1513.
Chipping Campden: C, L, ca, * 1401; C, L, 1450, 1467; C, 3L, 1484.
Cirencester: (C, L), c 1400; M, ca, * 1438; C, L, ca, * 1440; C, 4L, 1442; sym, c 1475 (128); M, L, L, 1462; (C), L, c 1470; E, 1478, c 1480; C, L, c 1480; (L), c 1480; (C), L, L, 1497; C, c 1500; C, L, sym, c 1500 (128; L, L, c 1530; C, 1587; C, L, 1626.
Coaley, Stroud: E, 1630.
Daylesford, Stow-on-the-Wold (formerly Worcs): C, 1632.
Deerhurst, Tewkesbury: Judge, L, ca, SS, * 1400 (106, 126, 135, 138, 61); L, c 1520, 1525.
Dowdeswell, Cheltenham: E, c 1520.
Doynton, Bristol: C, L, 1529.
Dyrham, Bristol: M, L, ca, * 1401 (85, 154, 33).
Eastington, Northleach: L, her, 1518.
Fairford, Lechlade: M, L, 1500; M, L, L, her, 1534, 1534.
Gloucester, Cathedral: Many indents.
— St John the Baptist: C, L, c 1520.
— St Mary de Crypt: L, L, 1519; C, L, SS, * 1529.
Kempsford, Lechlade: C, L, 1521.
Lechlade: C, L, c 1450; C, c 1510.
Leckhampton, Cheltenham: C, L, 1598.
Mitcheldean, Cinderford: L, L, c 1500.
Minchinhampton, Stroud: C, L, c 1500; S, c 1510; C, L, 1519.
Newent: M, 1523.
Newland, Coleford: M, L, 1443.
Northleach: C, L, * c 1400 (110); C, C, L, ca, * 1447 (110, 138, 88a); C, ca, * 1458 (70); C, L, c 1485, c 1490; Children, 1508; C, L, 1501; C, L, ca*, 1526; E, 1530; ins, 1584 (146).
Olveston, Bristol: M, M, her, 1505.
Rodmarton, Cirencester: C, 1461.
Sevenhampton, Cheltenham: C, 1497.
Thornbury: L, 1571.
Todenham, Moreton-in-the-Marsh: C, L, 1614.
Tormarton, Bristol: C, 1493.
Weston-sub-Edge, Chipping Campden: C, 1590.
Whittington, Cheltenham: C, L, 1560.
Winterbourne, Bristol: L, * c 1370.
Wormington, Evesham: L in bed, 1605 (45, 111, 147).
Wotton-under-Edge: M, L*, 1392 (89).
Yate, Bristol: C, L, L, 1590.

## HAMPSHIRE

Alton: L, c 1510; Children, c 1510.
Basingstoke: C, L, 1606; Child, 1621.
— Trinity Chapel (ruined): altar-tombs 1536 (20).
Bishop's Sutton, Alresford: M, L, c 1520.
Bramley, Basingstoke: C, 1452; L, 1504; C, L, 1529.
Bramshott, Liphook: C, L, c 1430.

ISLE OF WIGHT

Freshwater: M, * c 1365 (69).
Kingston: C, 1535.
Shorwell: E, 1518; L, 1619.


HEREFORDSHIRE


Brampton Abbots, Ross: L, 1506.
Burghill, Credenhill: C, L, 1616; sym, 1619.
Clehonger, Hereford: M, L, * c 1470.
Colwall, Ledbury: M, L, 1590.
Hereford Cathedral: Saint, 1282 (12, 34, 59, 135, 7); Bishop, * 1360 (92, 41); E, +, 1386; C, 1394 (99, 51); (E), 1428, 1434; M, L, ca, * 1435; ins, 1474 (147); E, SS, ca, 1476; C, 1480 (123); M, c 1480; ca, 1489; (E), 1490; M, L, L, 1514; E, c 1520; SS, ca, * 1524 (42, 127, 128, 14); E, SS, ca, * 1529 (127); many fragments; IS, 1497 (42, 110).
Kinnersley, Willersley: E, 1421.
Ledbury: Ac, c 1410; M, 1490, 1614.
Llandinabo, Hereford: Child, 1629 (46, 18).
Ludford, Ludlow: M, L, 1554 (73).
Lugwardine, Hereford: L, 1622.
Marden, Hereford: L, 1614.
Sollars Hope, Hereford: IS, c 1225 (32, 80, 81).
Weston-under-Penyard, Ross: C, 1609.


HERTFORDSHIRE


Abbot's Langley, Hemel Hempstead: L, L, 1498; C, L, L, 1607.
Albury, Standon: M, L, c 1475; C, L, 1588; M, L, 1592.
Aldbury, Tring: C, 1478; M, L, her, * 1547.
Aldenham, Watford: C, L, c 1520; C, c 1520; C, L, c 1520; C, c 1520; C, L, L, c 1525; (L), c 1525; L, c 1535, 1538; S, 1547; C, L, 1608.
Amwell, Great, Ware: Friar, c 1440 (94); stolen in 1968; C, L, L, c 1490.
Ardeley, Buntingford: (L), c 1420; E, 1515; C, L, 1599.
Aspenden, Buntingford: C, L, 1500; M, L, her, 1508.
Aston, Stevenage: Yeoman-of-the-Guard, L, 1592.
Baldock: L, c 1410; C, L, c 1420; S, c 1480; C, L, c 1480.
Barkway, Royston: C, L, L, 1561.
Barley, Royston: E, 1621.
Bayford, Hertford: M, (L), c 1545; M, c 1530.
Benington, Stevenage: E, c 1420.
Berkhampstead, Great: C, L, (ca), * 1356; M, c 1365; L, c 1370; E, c 1400; C, 1485; S, 1520; ins, pal, 1558/1500.
Braughing, Standon: C, L, c 1480; (L), c 1490; L, 1561.
Brent Pelham, Buntingford: L, L, 1627.
Broxbourne, Hoddesdon: E, c 1470; M, L, her, * 1473; E, c 1510; Sergeant-at-arms, L, 1531.
Buckland, Buntingford: L, 1451; E, 1478; C, 1499.
Buntingford: E, * 1620 (44).
Cheshunt: ca, 1448; C, 1449; L, 1453, 1502, 1609.
Clothall, Baldock: E, 1404, 1519, c 1535, 1602; L, 1578.
Digswell, Welwyn: M, L, * 1415 (122, 138); M, 1442; S, 1484; C, L, 1495, c 1530.
Eastwick, Harlow: L, 1564.

Broughton, Huntingdon: (C), c 1490.
Diddington, St Neots: (M), L, her, ca, SS, * 1505; L, SS, 1513.
Godmanchester: C, c 1520.
Offard Darcy, Godmanchester: M, L, L, c 1440; Ac, c 1530.
Sawtry, All Saints: M, L, * 1404.
Somersham: E, c 1530.
Stilton, Sawtry: C, L, 1606; C, C, 1618.
Stukeley, Little, Huntingdon: C, c 1590.

KENT (excluding London area)

Acrise, Folkestone: L, 1601.
Addington, Wrotham: M, 1378; M, L, ca, * 1409; M, c 1415, c 1445; E, 1446;
    M, L, 1470.
Aldington, Ashford: M, L, 1475.
Appledore, Tenterden: Child, c 1520.
Ash, Sandwich: L, ca, 1455; L, 1455; C, L, 1525; M, L, 1602; C, L, 1642.
Ash, Wrotham: E, 1465, 1605.
Ashford: (E), c 1320; L, ca, * 1375 (38, 59, 122, 126, *12*, *13*); (M), sym, 1490 (137).
Aylesford, Maidstone: M, L, 1426.
Barham, Canterbury: C, 1375; M, L, c 1455.
Bearstead, Maidstone: C, L, 1634.
Bethersden, Tenterden: C, 1459, 1591.
Biddenden, Tenterden: L, C, C, 1520; M, L, 1566; C, pal, 1572; C, L, L, 1584;
    C, 3L, 1593; C, L, L, 1598, 1609; C, L, 1628, 1641 (104).
Birchington, Margate: C, 1449, 1454; L, 1518; E, 1523; L, 1528, 1533.
Birling, Maidstone: C, 1522.
Bobbing, Sittingbourne: M, L, (ca), * c 1420; M, ca, * 1420.
Borden, Sittingbourne: C, c 1450; E, 1521.
Boughton Malherbe, Charing: C, L, 1499; M, L, 1529.
Boughton-under-Blean, Faversham: C, L, 1508; M, 1587; C, L, 1591.
Boxley, Maidstone: Ac, 1451; M, L, 1576.
Brabourne, Ashford: M, ca, * 1433; L, 1450; M, 1424; L, 1528.
Bredgar, Sittingbourne: Ac, 1518.
Brenchley, Tunbridge Wells: C, 3L, 1517; C, L, c 1540.
Brookland, Lydd: E, 1503.
Canterbury, Cathedral: Many indents (61, 93).
— St Alphege: Ac, 1523.
— St George: E, 1438.
— St Gregory Northgate: C, 1522.
— St Margaret: C, 1470.
— St Martin: C, L, 1587; M, 1591.
— St Paul: C, L, 1581.
Capel-le-Ferne, Folkestone: C, L, 1526.
Challock, Ashford: C, L, 1504.
Chart, Great, Ashford: C, c 1470; C, L, 1485; C, 5L, 1499; C, L, 1500; M, L, L, 1513;
    M, L, 1565; M, 1680 (51, 88, 138, *21*).
Chartham, Canterbury: M, * 1306 (23, 24, 27, 66, 79, 80, 117, 120, *4b*); E, 1416,
    1454, 1508; L, 1530.
Cheriton, Folkestone: Ac, 1474; E, 1502; L, 1592; M, 1915 (88).
Chevening, Sevenoaks: E, 1596.
Cliffe-at-Hoo, Rochester: C, L, L, 1609, 1652.

Lydd: Ac, 1420 (109, *64*); C, 1429; C, L, ca, * 1430; C, 1508, c 1520; C, L, 1557, 1566; C, 1578, c 1590; L, c 1590; C, 1608.
Lynsted, Sittingbourne: L, 1567; C, L, 1621; monument by E. Evesham (76).
Maidstone, All Saints: C, L, L, ancestors, 1593; C, L, 1640.
Maidstone Museum: E, c 1440, c 1450, c 1520; L, c 1550.
Malling, East, Maidstone: C, L, 1479 (101, *54*); E, 1522.
Malling, West, Maidstone: C, 1497, 1532; L, 1543.
Margate, St John: C, 1421; heart, 1433 (140); C, L, 1441; C, 1442; M, 1445; S, 1446; (L), 1475; E, 1515; ins, pal, 1582; M, c 1590; ship, 1615 (141, *90*).
Mereworth, Maidstone: M, ca, * 1366 (66, 69, *24*); C, L, 1479; C, sym, 1542 (130).
Mersham, Ashford: E, c 1420; C, L, c 1520.
Milton, Sittingbourne: M, c 1470; M, L, her, c 1500; L, 1529.
Minster, Isle of Sheppey: M, * French, c 1330 (58, 61, 115, *72*); L, * French, c 1336 (115).
Monkton, Isle of Thanet: E, c 1460.
Murston, Sittingbourne (old church): M, L, 1488.
Newington, Folkestone: L, c 1480; S, L, 1501; E, 1501; C, 3L, 1522; C, c 1570; M, L, 1630; Child, 1631.
Newington, Sittingbourne: C, C, 1488; L, 1580; C, L, L, 1581; L, 1600.
Northfleet, Gravesend: E, * 1375, 1391; M, L, 1433.
Otham, Maidstone: C, L, L, L, 1590.
Otterden, Faversham: M, * 1408; L, 1488; M, 1502, 1508; L, 1606.
Peckham, East, Tonbridge: C, L, c 1525.
Peckham, West, Tonbridge: L, c 1460.
Pembury, Tunbridge Wells: Child, 1607.
Penshurst, Tonbridge: C, L, 1514; +, c 1520 (132); many ins and fragments.
Pluckley, Ashford: M, 1425, 1440, 1517; M, L, 1517; L, 1526; M, 1545; M, her, 1550; M, L, 1610; mostly restored c 1630 (58).
Preston, Faversham: M, L, 1442; M, 1459; L, 1612.
Rainham, Gillingham: M, 1514; C, 1529; L, c 1530; C, L, c 1580.
Ringwould, Deal: L, 1505; C, 1530.
Rochester Cathedral: many indents (61).
Rochester, St Margaret: E, pal, 1465.
Romney, New: C, 1510; C, L, 1610.
Romney, Old: C, L, 1526.
St Lawrence, Thanet: M, 1444; L, 1493.
St Mary-in-the-Marsh, Romney: L, 1499; C, 1502.
St Nicholas-at-Wade, Thanet: C, L, L, 1574.
St Peter, Thanet: C, L, 1485, 1503.
Saltwood, Folkestone: E, 1370; M, L, * 1437; sym, 1496.
Sandwich, St Clement: C, ca, 1490.
Seal, Sevenoaks: M, * 1395 (40, 64, title page); C, pal, 1577/c 1500.
Selling, Faversham: Children, c 1520; C, c 1525.
Sheldwich, Faversham: M, L, ca, * 1394; M, L, 1426; S, 1431.
Shorne, Gravesend: C, L, 1457; L, c 1470; chalice, 1519; L, 1583.
Snodland, Maidstone: (C), 1441; C, 1486; C, L, 1487; C, L, L, 1530.
Southfleet, Gravesend: L, br, 1414; C, L, 1420; +, c 1420; E, 1456; S, c 1520; C, L, c 1520 (15).
Staple, Canterbury: C, c 1510.
Staplehurst, Cranbrook: L, c 1580.
Stockbury, Sittingbourne: C, L, 1617; L, 1648.
Stoke, Isle-of-Grain: E, 1415.
Stone, Dartford: E, +, * 1408 (132); ins, 1574 (123, 145, *77*).
Stourmouth, Canterbury: Ac, 1472.
Sundridge, Sevenoaks: M, 1429; C, c 1460; M, L, 1518.

Sutton, East, Maidstone: M, L, ** 1629 (76, 88).
Teynham, Sittingbourne: M, 1444; C, 1509, 1533; C, L, 1639.
Thanington, Canterbury: M, 1485.
Tilmanstone, Deal: C, L, 1598.
Trottescliffe, Wrotham: C, L, 1483.
Tudeley, Tonbridge: C, L, 1457.
Tunstall, Sittingbourne: E, 1525; L, c 1590.
Ulcombe, Maidstone: M, ca, * 1419; M, 1442; M, L, * 1470 (86, 35).
Upchurch, Gillingham: C, L, c 1350.
Westerham, Sevenoaks: C, L, L, 1511; C, L, 1529; C, 1531; 1533; C, L, L, 1557,
    1566; E, 1567.
Westwell, Ashford: IS, c 1320 (40).
Wittersham, Tenterden: C, 1523.
Woodchurch, Tenterden: E, +, * 1333 (132, 142, 148, 83); M, L, 1558.
Wouldham, Rochester: C, L, 1602.
Wrotham: C, L, 1498; C, c 1500; M, L, 1512; M, L, her, 1525; C, 1532; M, L, 1611;
    L, 1615.


LANCASHIRE

Childwall, Liverpool: M, L, her, 1524.
Eccleston, Preston: E, c 1510.
Flixton, Manchester: M, L, L, 1602.
Lancaster, St Mary: C, 1639.
Manchester Cathedral: E, ca, 1458; (M, L), ca, 1460; ca, c 1480; Bishop, 1515; M, L,
    c 1540; C, L, 1607, 1630.
Middleton: M, L, c 1510; E, 1522; L, M, M, 1531; C, L, 1618; M, L, 1650 (88).
Newchurch, Warrington: Children, 1561.
Ormskirk, Southport: M, her, * c 1500.
Preston: C, 1623.
Rivington, Wigan: S, 1627.
Rochdale: Five nineteenth-century forgeries.
Rufford, Southport: M, 1543.
Sefton, Liverpool: L, ca, 1528; M, L, L, 1568, * c 1570.
Ulveston: C, L, 1606.
Walton-on-the-Hill, Liverpool: C, 1586.
Whalley, Clitheroe: M, L, 1515.
Winwick, Warrington: M, her, ca, * 1492; M/E, L, * 1527 (147).


LEICESTERSHIRE

Aylestone, Leicester: E, 1594.
Barwell: E, L, 1614; C, L, 1659.
Bottesford: E, SS, * 1404; (E), c 1440.
Castle Donington: M, L, ca, * 1458.
Hoby, Melton Mowbray: (M), c 1480.
Launde, Oakham: M, L, 1458.
Leicester, Wigston's Hospital Chapel: S, c 1540.
Loughborough: (C, L), 1445; C, L, 1480.
Lutterworth: C, L, 1418, c 1470.
Melton Mowbray: Heart, 1543.
Packington, Ashby-de-la-Zouch: E, c 1530, stolen in 1968.
Queeniborough, Leicester: L, 1634.

Saxelby, Melton Mowbray: L, 1523.
Scalford, Melton Mowbray: C, 1520.
Sheepshed: M, L, 1592.
Sibstone, Nuneaton: E, sym, * 1532.
Stapleford, Melton Mowbray: M, L, 1492.
Stockerston, Uppingham: (M), L, * 1467; M, L, 1493.
Swithland, Loughborough: L, c 1455.
Thurcaston, Leicester: E, ca, * 1425.
Wanlip, Leicester: M, L, * 1393.
Wymondham, Melton Mowbray: L, 1521.

### LINCOLNSHIRE

Algarkirk, Boston: C, L, L, SS, 1498.
Althorpe, Scunthorpe: E, c 1360.
Ashby Puerorum, Horncastle: M, L, c 1560; M, c 1560; IS, E, c 1320.
Barrowby, Grantham: C, L, 1479; (M), L, her, 1508.
Barton-on-Humber, St Mary: L, c 1380; C, * 1433.
Barton-on-Humber, St Peter: (M), c 1440.
Bigby, Barnetby: L, c 1520; E, L, 1632.
Boston, St Botolph: C, ca, SS, * 1398; E, SS, * c 1400; (C), L, L, c 1400; C, 1659;
   many fragments, indents, incised slabs (40, 63).
Broughton, Brigg: M, L, ca, * c 1390.
Burton Coggles, Grantham: C, c 1590; M, L, c 1620.
Burton Pedwardine, Sleaford: L, 1631.
Buslingthorpe, Market Rasen: M, * c 1300 (34, 80, 27). Soon to be moved to
   Spridlington.
Coates, Great, Grimsby: L, c 1420; C, L, 1503.
Coates-by-Stow, Gainsborough: M, L, 1590, 1602.
Conisholme, Saltfleet: M, L, 1515.
Corringham, Gainsborough: E, L, 1628.
Covenham St Bartholomew, Saltfleet: M, 1415.
Croft, Skegness: M, * c 1300 (34, 80).
Driby, Alford: (C), L, 1583.
Edenham, Bourne: SS, c 1500.
Evedon, Sleaford: C, L, 1630.
Fiskerton, Lincoln: E, c 1490.
Gedney, Holbeach: L, ca, sym, SS, ** 1390.
Glentham, Market Rasen: L, 1452.
Grainthorpe, Saltfleet: +, * c 1380 (132).
Gunby, Skegness: M, L, ca, c 1400; Judge, ca, * 1419.
Hainton, Market Rasen: C, L, 1435; M, L, her, 1553.
Halton Holgate, Spilsby: L, 1658.
Harpswell, Gainsborough: M, L, c 1480.
Harrington, Spilsby: L, 1480; M, L, 1585.
Holbeach: (M), c 1410; L, 1488.
Horncastle: M, 1519; S, 1519.
Ingoldmells, Skegness: C, 1520.
Irnham, Bourne: M, ca, * 1390; M, c 1440.
Kelsey, South, Caistor: M, L, c 1410.
Laughton, Gainsborough: M, ca, * c 1400.
Lincoln Minster: Mitre, 1494 (71); Many indents, some very early (33, 58, 63).
— St Benedict: C, L, 1620.
— St Mary-le-Wigford: +, 1468; ins, 1525 (141, 147).

Linwood, Market Rasen: C, L, ca, ** 1419; C, ca, * 1421.
Mablethorpe: L, 1522.
Northorpe, Boston: C, L, L, 1595.
Norton Disney, Newark: M, L, M, L, L, 1578.
Ormesby, South, Alford: L, c 1410; M, L, ca, 1482.
Pinchbeck, Spalding: L, 1608.
Rand, Lincoln: (M), c 1500; L, L, 1590.
Rauceby, Sleaford: E, 1536.
Scotter, Kirton: C, L, 1599.
Scrivelsby, Horncastle: M, 1545.
Sleaford: C, L, 1521.
Somersby, Horncastle: C, 1612.
Spalding, Johnson Hospital: C, L, 1597 (in boardroom).
Spilsby: L, * 1391; M, L, ca, ** c 1400.
Stallingborough, Grimsby: M, L, her, 1509; L, 1610.
Stamford, All Saints: C, L,* 1460; C, L, ca, * c 1465: L, 1471; C, L, 1475, c 1500; E, 1508.
Stamford, St John: C, L, 1489; E, 1497.
Stamford, St Mary: C, 1684.
Stoke Rocheford, Grantham: M, 1470; M, L, 1503.
Tattershall, Coningsby: C, 1411; E, 1456; (M), ca, SS, * c 1470 (89, 139); L, ca, SS, * 1470, ** c 1475 (135); E, SS, * c 1510; E, 1519.
Theddlethorpe, All Saints, Mablethorpe: M, 1424.
Waltham, Grimsby: L, 1420.
Wickenby, Market Rasen: S, 1635.
Winterton, Scunthorpe: L, L, 1504.
Winthorpe, Skegness: C, L, 1505; C, 1515.
Witham, North, Colsterworth: (C), 1424.
Wrangle, Boston: C, L, 1503.

LONDON—METROPOLITAN AREA
(Former counties in brackets, since old books refer to these)

Acton, W.3 (Middlesex): C, 1558.
Addington, Croydon (Surrey): M, 1540; C, L, 1544.
Barking (Essex): Ac, c 1480; E, 1485; C, L, 1493, 1596.
Barnes, S.W.13 (Surrey): L, L, 1508.
Beckenham, Bromley (Kent): M, L, L, her, 1552; L, 1563.
Bedfont, Hounslow (Middlesex): C, 1631.
Beddington, Croydon (Surrey): L, 1414; +, 1425; C, L, ca, * 1432; C, L, c 1430; M, 1437; L, L, 1507; M, L, her (restored), 1520.
Bexley (Kent): Hunting horn, c 1450 (141); C, 1513.
Brentford, New, St Lawrence (Middlesex): C, L, 1528.
Bromley (Kent): C, L, L, 1600.
Camberwell, St Giles, S.E.5 (Surrey): C, 1497, 1499; M, L, 1532; M, 1538; C, L, 1570, 1577.
Carshalton, Sutton (Surrey): M, L, c 1480 (25); E, 1493; (M), ca, sym, 1497 (130, 82c); L, 1524.
Cheam, Sutton (Surrey): C, c 1390, c 1390; C, L, 1458; C, 1459; M, c 1475; C, L, sym, 1542.
Chelsea, Old Church, S.W.3 (Middlesex): L, her, 1555; M, L, 1625.
Chelsfield, Orpington (Kent): SS, 1417 (129); E, c 1420, c 1420; L, c 1480, 1510.
Chislehurst, Bromley (Kent): E, 1482.
Clapham, St Peter, S.W.4 (Surrey): E, c 1470.

M

### MONMOUTHSHIRE

Acle, Yarmouth: C, 1533; E, 1627.
Aldborough, Cromer: M, 1481; L, 1485; C, c 1490.
Antingham, North Walsham: M, L, 1562.
Attlebridge, Norwich: Chalice, c 1525.
Aylsham: E, c 1490; C, L, c 1490; S, 1499; C, L, c 1500; S, 1507.
Baconsthorpe, Cromer: L, her, 1561.
Barnham Broom, Dereham: C, 1467; C, L, 1514.
Barningham Northwood, Saxthorpe: M, L, 1516.
Barningham Winter, Saxthorpe: M, c 1410.
Bawburgh, Norwich: S, 1505; Chalice, 1531; S, 1660.
Beechamwell, Swaffham: E, c 1385, 1430.
Beeston Regis, Cromer: C, L, 1527 (111).
Belaugh, Norwich: Chalice, 1508.
Binham, Wells: C, L, c 1530.
Bintry, Fakenham: Chalice, 1510.
Blickling, Aylsham: C, c 1360; M, * 1401; C, L, 1454; L, 1458; Child, 1479; L, c 1485;
    L, Children, 1512.
Brampton, Aylsham: S, SS, 1468; M, L, L, 1535; C, L, 1622.
Brisley, Dereham: E, 1531.
Burgh St Margaret, Yarmouth: E, 1608.
Burlingham, South (St Edmund), Norwich: Chalice, 1540.
Burnham Thorpe, Brancaster: M, ca, * 1420.
Burnham Westgate, Brancaster: L, 1523.
Buxton, Aylsham: Chalice, 1508.
Bylaugh, Dereham: M, L, 1471.
Cley, Wells: C, c 1450, c 1460; S, 1512; E, c 1520.
Clippesby, Yarmouth: C, L, 1503; M, L, 1594.
Colney, Norwich: Chalice, 1502.
Creake, North, Fakenham: C, ca, c 1500.
Creake, South, Fakenham: E, c 1400, 1509 (96).
Cressingham, Great, Swaffham: M, L, 1497; C, L, 1509; E, 1518; (L), 1588.
Cromer: L, 1518.
Dereham, East: E, 1479; L, 1486; rebus, 1503 (123).
Ditchingham, Bungay: C, L, 1490; C, C, 1505.
Dunston, Norwich: C, S, 1649.
Ellingham, Great, Attleborough: L, c 1500.
Elsing, Dereham: M, ca, SS, ** 1347 (38, 66, 82, 84, 117, 135, 137, *31*).
Erpingham, Aylsham: M, * 1415.
Fakenham: E, 1428; (C), L, L, c 1470; Hearts, c 1470; L, c 1510.
Felbrigg, Cromer: L, * c 1380; M, L, ca, ** 1416 (90); L, c 1480; M, c 1608:
    L, 1608.
Feltwell, St Mary, Thetford: M, 1479; L, 1520.
Fincham, Swaffham: S, c 1520.
Fransham, Great, Swaffham: M, ca, * 1414; S, c 1500.
Frenze, Diss: M, 1475, 1510; L, 1519; S, c 1520; L, 1521; (M, L), 1551.
Frettenham, Norwich: L, c 1420, c 1460.
Gorleston, Yarmouth (formerly Suffolk): M, * c 1320 (81, *29*).
Guestwick, Fakenham: Chalice, 1504; C, 1505, c 1520.
Halvergate, Yarmouth: L, pal, 1540/c 1440 (96).
Harling, West, Thetford: E, 1479; M, L, c 1490, 1508.
Heacham, Hunstanton: M, c 1485.
Hedenham, Bungay: Chalice, 1502.
Heigham, near Norwich: C, 1630.

Stoke Bruerne, Towcester: E, 1625.
Sudborough, Kettering: C, L, 1415.
Sulgrave, Banbury: C, L, 1564.
Tansor, Oundle: E, 1440.
Wappenham, Towcester: M, c 1460; Judge, L, 1479; L, 1499; M, L, c 1500, c 1500.
Warkworth, Banbury: (M), 1412; M, 1420; L, 1420, 1430; M, 1454.
Welford, Market Harborough: M, 3L, 1585.
Woodford-cum-Membris, Daventry: E, c 1420.
Woodford, Thrapston: M, 1480.


NORTHUMBERLAND

Newcastle-on-Tyne, All Saints: C, L, ca, SS, Flemish, ** 1411 (59, 114).


NOTTINGHAMSHIRE

Annesley, Mansfield: Huntsman, 1595 (in Hall).
Clifton, East Retford: M, 1478, 1491; C, L, 1587.
Darlton, East Retford: M, L, c 1510.
Hickling, Melton Mowbray: E, 1521.
Markham, East, East Retford: L, * 1419.
Newark-on-Trent: C, ca, SS, Flemish, ** 1361 (114); C, c 1540, 1557; many ins.
Ossington, Newark: M, L, 1551.
Radcliffe-on-Trent, Nottingham: L, 1626.
Southwell Minster: About 25 ins.
Stanford-on-Soar, Loughborough: E, c 1400.
Strelley, Nottingham: M, L, * 1487.
Wollaton, Nottingham: M, L, * 1471.


OXFORDSHIRE

Adderbury, Banbury: M, L, c 1460; L, 1508 (153).
Alvescot, Bampton: C, L, 1579.
Aston Rowant, Thame: C, L, 1445; (L), c 1470, 1508.
Bampton: E, c 1420, 1500; L, 1633.
Barford, Great, Banbury: C, L, 1495.
Beckley, Oxford: L, 1619.
Bicester: C, L, c 1510.
Brightwell Baldwin, Watlington: ins in English, c 1370; Judge, L, * 1439 (two).
Brightwell Salome, Watlington: E, 1492.
Broughton, Banbury: L, 1414.
Burford: C, L, br, 1437; C, 1609 (in churchyard); C, L, 1614.
Cassington, Eynsham: +, * 1414; S, 1590.
Caversfield, Bicester: C, 1435; L, 1506; Heart, 1533.
Chalgrove, Dorchester: M, 1441; M, L, L, 1446.
Charlton-on-Otmoor, Bicester: E, 1476.
Chastleton, Chipping Norton: L, 1592; C, L, 1613.
Checkendon, Wallingford: C, ca, * 1404; sym, 1430; L, 1490.
Chesterton, Bicester: C, L, 1612.
Chinnor, Thame: E, +, * c 1320; Ac, 1361; M, L, L, 1385; M, L, c 1385; E, 1388;
    L, c 1390, 1392; (C, L), c 1410; C, c 1410; M, c 1430; C, L, L, 1514.

N

— Ashmolean Museum: L, c 1530; large collection of rubbings.
Pyrton, Watlington: C, L, 1522; IS, c 1325 (40).
Rollright, Great, Chipping Norton: E, 1522.
Rotherfield-Greys, Henley: M, ca, * 1387.
Shiplake, Henley: C, L, c 1540.
Shipton-under-Wychwood, Burford: S, 1548.
Shirburn, Watlington: M, L, 1496.
Somerton, Bicester: M, L, pal, 1552 (73).
Souldern, Banbury: Heart, c 1460; E, 1514; C, c 1580.
Southleigh, Witney: C, 1557.
Stadhampton, Dorchester: C, L, 1498, 1508.
Stanton Harcourt, Eynsham: C, C, 1460; L, 1516; E, 1519.
Steeple Aston, Bicester: C, L, 1522.
Stoke Lyne, Bicester: C, L, sym, 1535; C, L, 1582.
Stoke, North, Watlington: (E), 1363.
Stoke Talmage, Watlington: C, L, 1504; M, L, 1589.
Swinbrook, Burford: M, L, L, L, c 1470 (101, 53); M, her, 1510.
Tew, Great, Chipping Norton: M, L, ca, * 1410; sym, 1487; C, L, 1513.
Thame: M, L, M, L, br, * c 1420 (71); M, L, M, 1460; C, L, c 1500; C, L, L, 1502;
     C, L, 1503, 1508; M, her, 1539; C, 1543, 1597.
Waterperry, Oxford: L, c 1370; M, L, pal, c 1540/1442 (57); M, c 1530.
Watlington: C, L, 1485; S, 1501; C, 1588.
Whitchurch, Pangbourne: M, L, c 1420; E, c 1455, 1610.
Witney: C, L, L, 1500; C, 1606.
Woodstock: C, 1441; E, 1631.


### RUTLAND


Braunston, Oakham: C, L, 1596.
Casterton, Little, Stamford: M, L, * c 1410.
Lyddington, Uppingham: L, 1486; C, L, 1530.


### SHROPSHIRE


Acton Burnell, Much Wenlock: M, ca, * 1382.
Acton Scott, Church Stretton: C, L, 1571.
Adderley, Market Drayton: Bishop, * c 1390; M, L, c 1560.
Alveley, Bridgnorth: C, 1616.
Burford, Ludlow: L, c 1370.
Drayton: C, c 1580.
Edgemond, Newport: S, L, 1533.
Glazeley, Bridgnorth: C, L, 1599.
Harley, Much Wenlock: M, L, 1475.
Ightfield, Whitchurch: L, ca, SS, c 1495; C, 1497.
Myddle, Shrewsbury: C, L, 1564.
Newport: 41 ins (52).
Plowden Hall (private chapel), Bishop's Castle: C, L, 1557.
Shrewsbury, St Alkmund: L, c 1500.
Tong, Oakengates: M, L, * 1467; E, 1510; Ac, 1517.
Upton Cresset, Bridgnorth: C, L, 1640.
Wenlock, Much: C, L, 1592.
Withington, Shrewsbury: M, L, 1512; E, 1530.

Blore-Ray, Ashbourne: C, L, 1498.
Clifton-Campville, Tamworth: L, br, c 1360.
Eccleshall: L, 1672.
Hanbury, Burton-on-Trent: E, c 1480.
Horton, Biddulph: C, L, 1589.
Kinver, Kidderminster: M, 1528.
Leek: C, 4L, 1597.
Madeley, Newcastle-under-Lyme: C, L, 1518; C, 1586.
Norbury, Newport: L, ca, * 1360.
Okeover, Ashbourne: M, L, L, ca, pal, * 1538/1447.
Rugeley: C, 1566.
Standon, Eccleshall: +, c 1420.
Stone: M, L, 1619.
Trantham, Stoke-on-Trent: M, L, 1591.


SUFFOLK


Acton, Long Melford: M, ** c 1310 (15, 35, 65, 79, 161, 8); L, ca, * 1435; M, 1528; C, L, 1589; C, 1598 (144).
Aldeburgh: (C), 1519; L, c 1520, c 1570 (144); C, L, 1601, 1606; C, 1612; C, L, L, 1635.
Ampton, Bury St Edmunds: C, L, c 1480; L, c 1480, c 1491; Children, c 1490.
Ash Bocking, Needham Market: M, L, L, 1585.
Assington, Nayland: M, L, c 1500.
Barham, Ipswich: C, L, 1514.
Barningham, Thetford: Ac, 1499.
Barrow, Bury St Edmunds: M, L, L, 1570.
Barsham, Beccles: M, c 1415.
Belstead, Ipswich: M, L, L, 1518.
Bergholt, East, Nayland: C, 1639.
Bildeston, Hadleigh: L, 1599.
Boxford, Nayland: Child, 1606.
Bradley, Little, Haverhill: C, L, c 1510; M, c 1530; C, L, 1584, 1605; M, L, 1612.
Braiseworth (old church), Eye: M, 1569.
Bredfield, Wickham Market: C, L, 1611.
Bruisyard, Yoxford: L, L, 1611.
Brundish, Stradbroke: E, c 1360; M, 1559; M, L, 1560, c 1570; C, 1571.
Burgate, Eye: M, L, ca, * 1409.
Bury St Edmunds, St Mary: C, L, c 1480; E, 1514; many ins.
Campsey Ash, Wickham Market: E, ca, 1504.
Carlton, Saxmundham: C, c 1480, c 1490.
Chattisham, Ipswich: L, 1592.
Cookley, Halesworth: C, L, 1595.
Cowlinge, Haverhill: C, L, 1599.
Debenham: M, L, c 1425.
Denham, Eye: C, 1574.
Denstone, Haverhill: M, L, her, 1524, L, c 1530.
Depden, Bury St Edmunds: L, L, M, M, 1572.
Easton, Wickham Market: M, c 1425, 1584; L, 1601 (104, 58).
Edwardstone, Sudbury: C, L, 1636.
Ellough, Beccles: L, c 1520, 1607.
Elmham, South, (St James), Halesworth: C, L, c 1500.
Euston, Thetford: C, L, c 1480, c 1520; L, c 1530; M, L, L, c 1530.
Eyke, Woodbridge: Judge, L, c 1430; E, 1619.

Stoke-by-Nayland: L, c 1400; M, * 1408; L, her, 1535; Children, c 1590; L, 1632; fragments.
Stonham Aspall, Debenham: E, 1606.
Stowmarket: S, 1638.
Stratford St Mary, Nayland: C, L, 1558.
Tannington, Stradbroke: L, 1612.
Thurlow, Great, Haverhill: M, L, c 1460; L, c 1460; M, L, c 1530.
Thurlow, Little, Haverhill: M, L, c 1520.
Ufford, Woodbridge: (C), 3L, 1488; S, 1598.
Walberswick, Southwold: many indents (58).
Waldingfield, Little, Sudbury: C, L, 1506; M, L, 1526; L, c 1530; C, 1544.
Walton, Felixstowe: C, L, 1459; C, 1612.
Wenham, Little, Nayland: M, L, 1514.
Wickhambrook, Haverhill: C, L, L, 1597.
Wickham Skeith, Stradbroke: L, c 1530.
Wilby, Stradbroke: C, c 1530.
Woodbridge: C, 1601.
Worlingham, Beccles: C, L, 1511.
Worlingworth, Stradbroke: Children, c 1520.
Wrentham: L, 1400; M, 1493.
Yaxley, Eye: C, 1598.
Yoxford: M, L, 1428 (70); S, * 1485 (113, *68*); C, 1613; L, 1618, 1618.


SURREY (excluding London area)

Albury (old church), Guildford: M, 1440.
Ashford, Sunbury (formerly Middlesex): C, L, 1522.
Betchworth, Reigate: E, 1533.
Bletchingley, Godstone: L, c 1470; E, c 1510; Children, c 1520; C, L, sym, 1541.
Bookham, Great, Leatherhead: L, 1433, 1597; C, L, 1598; C, 1668.
Byfleet, Weybridge: E, c 1480.
Charlwood, Horley: M, L, 1553.
Chipstead, Banstead: L, 1614.
Cobham: Sym, c 1500 (129); M, pal, 1550/c 1510.
Compton, Guildford: C, L, 1508.
Cranleigh: Sym, 1503; E, c 1510.
Crowhurst, Lingfield: M, 1450, 1460; cast-iron slab, 1591 (48, *20*).
Egham, Staines: C, L, L, 1576.
Ewell: L, her, 1519; L, 1521, 1577.
Farnham: C, L, 1594; L, 1597.
Godalming: C, L, 1509; M, 1595.
Godalming, Wyatt's Almshouse Chapel: C, L, 1619.
Guildford, Holy Trinity: C, c 1500; C, L, 1607.
— St Mary: C, L, c 1500.
— St Nicholas: C, 1676.
— Surrey Archaeological Society: M, L, c 1500 (55).
Horley: L, ca, * c 1420 (59, 125, *78*); C, c 1510.
Horsell, Woking: C, 1603, 1603; C, L, 1619.
Horsley, East, Guildford: C, c 1390; bishop, 1478 (72, 120, *25*); C, L, 1498; Children, 1504.
Leatherhead: C, c 1470.
Leigh, Reigate: C, L, 1449; L, c 1450; sym, 1499.
Lingfield: L, * 1375 (98); M, * 1403; M, 1417; L, ca, 1420 (71, 122, 126, *79*); L, c 1420 (100); E, c 1440, 1445; L, c 1450; E, 1458, 1469, 1503. Incised tiles (29).

### SUSSEX

Winchelsea: C, c 1440.
Wiston, Steyning: M, * 1426.
Worthing Museum: E, c 1440 (70).

## WARWICKSHIRE

Astley, Bedworth: (L), c 1400.
Aston, Birmingham: Judge, 1545.
Baddesley-Clinton Hall, Atherstone: L, her, c 1520.
Baginton, Coventry: M, L, her, * 1407.
Barcheston, Shipston-on-Stour: Ac, 1530.
Barton, Bidford-on-Avon: C, L, 1608.
Chadshunt, Kineton: C, 1613.
Clifford Chambers, Stratford (formerly Glos): M, L, 1583; L, 1601.
Compton Verney, Kineton: L, 1523; M, L, 1526; M, c 1630.
Coughton, Alcester: M, L, her, c 1535.
Coventry Cathedral: several brasses destroyed (21, 54).
Coventry, Holy Trinity: C, L, L, 1600 (27).
Exhall, Alcester: M, L, c 1590.
Hampton-in-Arden: C, c 1500.
Haseley, Warwick: M, L, 1573.
Hillmorton, Rugby: L, c 1410.
Hunningham, Leamington: Children, c 1450.
Long Itchington, Leamington: C, L, L, 1674.
Lower Quinton, Stratford (formerly Glos): L, ca, * c 1430.
Merevale, Atherstone: M, L, * 1413.
Meriden, Hampton-in-Arden: L, 1638.
Middleton, Tamworth: Judge, L, 1476.
Preston-Bagot, Warwick: L, 1635.
Solihull: C, L, L, 1549; C, L, 1610.
Stratford-on-Avon: ins, Anne Shakespeare, 1623.
Sutton Coldfield: L, 1606; C, 1621.
Tamworth: L, 1614.
Tysoe, Banbury: E, 1463; L, 1598.
Ufton, Leamington: E, L, 1587.
Upper Shuckburgh, Daventry: (L), c 1500; M, L, 1549, 1594.
Warwick, St Mary: M, L, her, * 1406; C, L, 1573.
Warwick, St Nicholas: E, 1424.
Wellesbourne-Hastings, Stratford: M, 1426.
Weston-upon-Avon, Stratford (formerly Glos): M, her, 1546, 1559.
Whatcote, Shipston-on-Stour: E, 1511.
Whichford, Chipping Norton: E, 1582.
Whitnash, Leamington: C, L, c 1500; E, 1531.
Withybrook, Coventry: C, c 1500.
Wixford, Alcester: M, L, ca, * 1411; Child, 1597.
Wooton-Wawen, Alcester: M, L, 1505.
Wroxhall, Kenilworth: L, c 1430.

## WESTMORLAND

Kendal: M, 1577.
Morland, Appleby: ins, pal, 1562.
Musgrave, Great, Kirkby Stephen: E, c 1500.

Sessay, Thirsk, N.R.: E, 1550.
Sheriff Hutton, Easingwold, N.R.: Children, 1491; L, 1657.
Sledmore, Driffield, E.R.: M, 1915 (53, 88).
Sprotborough, Doncaster, W.R.: M, L, 1474.
Tanfield, West, Ripon, N.R.: E, c 1490.
Thirsk, N.R.: E, 1419.
Thornton Watlass, Bedale, N.R.: S, 1669 (in churchyard).
Todwick, Sheffield, W.R.: C, 1609.
Topcliffe, Thirsk, N.R.: C, L, ca, SS, Flemish, ** 1391 (114).
Wath, Ripon, N.R.: Judge, L, 1420; M, c 1490.
Wellwick, Patrington, E.R.: C, L, 1621.
Wensley, Leyburn, N.R.: E, Flemish, * 1375 (115).
Wentworth, Barnsley, W.R.: M, L, 1588.
Wilberfosse, York, E.R.: M, L, 1447.
Winestead, Patrington, E.R.: M, L, c 1540.
Wycliffe, Barnard Castle, N.R.: C, 1606.
York, Minster: Archbishop, * 1315; L, 1585; C, 1595; many indents (58).
— All Saints, Pavement: C, 1597.
— St Martin, Coney Street: C, 1614.
— St Michael Spurriergate: Chalice, 1466.


SCOTLAND

Aberdeen, St Nicholas: C, Flemish, ** 1613 (30, 62, 115).
Edinburgh, St Giles: sym, 1569 (30).
Glasgow Cathedral: M, 1605.


WALES

Beaumaris, Anglesea: C, L, sym, SS, * 1530.
Bettws Cedewain, Newton, Montgomery: E, 1531.
Clynnog, Caernarvon: C, 1633.
Dolwyddelan, Caenarvon: M, L, 1525.
Haverfordwest, Pembroke: C, L, 1654.
Holt, Wrexham, Denbigh: S, 1666.
Llanbeblig, Caernarvon: C in bed, * 1500.
Llandough, Penarth, Glamorgan: L, ca, 1427.
Llangafelach, Swansea, Glamorgan: C, L, 1631.
Llanrwst, Denbigh: M, 1626; L, 1632, 1658; M, 1660; L, 1669, 1671.
Llanwenllwyfo, Pensarn, Anglesea: C, L, 1609.
Mold, Flint: C, 1602.
Ruthin, Denbigh: C, 1560; C, L, 1583.
St Davids Cathedral, Pembroke: M (restored), 1528.
Swansea, Glamorgan: M, L, sym, * c 1500.
Whitchurch, Denbigh: C, L, 1575.
Wrexham, Denbigh: S, 1673.
Yspytty-Ifan, Caernarvon: C, L, 1598.


EIRE

Bandon, Christ Church, Kilbrogan, Co Cork: ins, 1626.
Dublin, Christ Church Cathedral: Children, c 1580.
Dublin, St Patrick's Cathedral: E, sym, 1528 (55), 1537; C, L, 1579.

# SUBJECT INDEX

*(Italic numerals refer to figure numbers)*